LEARNING CENTERS

for open-ended activities

LEARNING CENTERS

written by
Liz and Dick Wilmes

A **BUILDING BLOCKS** Publication

38W567 Brindlewood, Elgin, IL 60123

ART

Cover Design and Art:

David Van Delinder
David Jensen *for*
STUDIO 155
Elgin, IL 60120

Text Illustrations:

Nel Gammon Webster

Typesetting and
Layout Mechanicals:

Greg Wilmes

SPECIAL THANKS TO

Vohny Moehling, Nancy Adams, Eric Wilmes for their patience, creative thinking, and editorial comments.

PUBLISHED BY:

38W567 Brindlewood
Elgin, Illinois 60123

DISTRIBUTED BY:

Gryphon House
P.O. Box 207
Beltsville, MD 20704

(Educational Stores & Catalogs)

Consortium Book Sales
1045 Westgate Drive
St. Paul, MN 55114

(U.S. Book Trade)

Monarch Books
5000 Dufferin St., Unit K
Downsview, Ontario
Canada M3H 5T5

(All Canadian Orders)

Dedicated to:

... teachers who support young children's natural curiosity, creativity, movement, and language.

CONTENTS

Art

Helps Children With:

Awareness
Creativity
Exploring Media
Language Development
Relaxation
Self Expression
Sense of Color & Design
Small Motor Control

Art
Paper List

Adding Machine Tape

Aluminum Foil

Blotters

Boxes

Butcher

Cardboard

Cardboard Tubes

Coffee Filters

Computer

Construction

Corrugated Board

Doilies

Easel

Fingerpaint

Freezer Wrap

Grocery Bags

Mailing

Manilla

Newsprint

Newspaper

Pizza Boards

Placemats

Plates

Sandpaper

Shelf

Tablecloths

Tissue

Towels

Wallpaper (both sides)

Watercolor

Waxed

Wrapping

Paint
Supply List

Paints

Tempera
   Cakes
   Fluorescent
   Powdered
   Pre-Mixed

Finger
   Glittering
   Pre-Mixed

Special
   Flour/Water Mixture
   Glass Wax
   Liquid Dish Soap
   Liquid Starch
   Mud
   Paste
   Shaving Cream
   Soap Flake/Water Mixture

Watercolors
   Foam Paint
   Food Coloring/Water Mixture
   Washable

Add 'Texture'

Baking Powder
Cornmeal
Cornstarch
Flour
Liquid Soap
Kosher Salt
Peppercorns
Sand
Sawdust
Soap Flakes
Sugar

Add 'Smell'

Cinnamon
Lemon Juice
Peppermint Extract
Vanilla Extract
Whole Cloves
Wintergreen Extract

Paint Clean-Up

Mop
Paper Towels
Soap
Sponges
Water

Paint With

Rollers
  Brayers
  Corn Cobs
  Deodorant Bottles
  Field Corn
  Furniture Casters
  Hair Rollers
  Paint Rollers
  Rolling Pins
  Toy Cars

Print-Making Tools
  Berry Baskets
  Blocks
  Cardboard Tubes
  Checkers
  Cookie Cutters
  Corks
  Dominoes
  Egg Cartons
  Jar Lids
  Kitchen Utensils
  Paper Cups
  Pumpkin Pieces
  Rind From Different Fruit
  Small Building Blocks
  Sponges
  Spools
  Wadded Newspaper Balls

Brushes
  Basting
  Bath
  Dish
  Easel
  Hair
  Household
  Paint
  Scrub
  Shoe Shine
  Sponge
  Tooth

Miscellaneous Items
  Evergreen Branches
  Eye Droppers
  Feather Dusters
  Fly Swatters
  Ice Cubes/Icicles
  Ketchup and Mustard
    Containers
  Scouring Pads
  Shoe Polish Applicator
  String
  Tree Branches
  Wide-Mouth, Plastic
    Straws

Paint On

Brownie Pans
Carpet Protector Strip
Chair and Desk Protector
Cookie Sheets
Fabric
Linoleum
Paper (See Pg. 10)

Pie Pans
Plastic Placemats
Plates
Rubber Shower Mats
Trays
Wood

At The Easel

EASEL MIX AND MATCH: Offer various paint brushes and tempera paint with all types of paper.

- Shoe polish applicators with several colors of tempera paint on corrugated cardboard which you've cut from large boxes.

- Easel brush with sand textured tempera paint on easel paper. EXTENSION: Add other textures on different days.
Encourage The Children: Ask the children if the paint seems different to them. "What is the difference?" Look at their paintings with them. Find places where their paintings seem most gritty.

- Narrow sponge brushes with several colors of tempera paint on one or two paper towel rolls. Remember to turn them around and paint the backsides.

- Easel brushes with several colors of tempera paint on butcher paper cut into large pennant shapes.
Encourage The Children: "Corrine, is it hard to paint in the point of the pennant?" "Look, you used all of the paint colors."

BUDDY PAINTING: Have several pairs of matching colored headbands near the easel. Encourage pairs of children to wear matching headbands and paint together.

- Cut the easel paper in half, clip both pieces to the same easel board and let children paint individually while standing next to each other.

- Clip one large sheet of paper to the easel. Encourage 2 children to paint together on the same piece of paper. Remember to write both children's names on their painting.
Encourage The Children: "How did you decide what each person would paint?"

SIT AND PAINT: Lower each of the easel boards to the shortest height. Put a chair by each board of the easel. Let the children choose whether to sit or stand as they paint.

TEMPERA PAINT MIX AND MATCH: Offer tempera paint, various brushes, and other tools on paper or other surfaces in a variety of ways.

- Scouring pads with whole clove textured paint on light colored plain paper. (It is easier for children to paint with scouring pads if you securely clip a clothespin to each one.)

- Wide paint brushes with paint on a large piece of plywood. After dry, drill holes in the top and hang it in the school entrance or hallway.

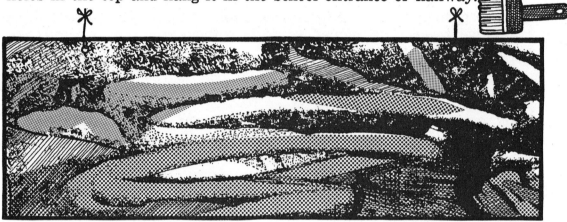

- Ice cubes or icicles with powdered tempera in salt shakers on paper plates. Have a child sprinkle the powdered tempera paint on his plate and then move the ice through the paint. Remember to wear mittens. Continue until the plate is full of color.
VARIATION: Get the plate wet by moving the ice all around it. Slowly sprinkle the powdered tempera paint on the wet plate.
Encourage The Children: Have the children go slowly so that they can watch the paint dissolve and mix. "What colors appear?"

GIANT PAINT MURALS: Use various brushes and other tools along with paint on large pieces of paper.

Using Brushes

- **Drop Paint** - Tape a long piece of newsprint to the table. Fill small plastic tubs about half full of different colors of tempera paint and put a paint brush in each one.

  Have a child stand close to the table, pick up a tub of paint in one hand, dip the brush into the paint, hold it over the paper, and watch the paint slide off of the brush dropping onto the paper. Continue.
  EXTENSION: Repeat, taping paper to the floor.
  Encourage The Children: Find the largest/smallest drops. Find 'piggyback' drops. Find funny looking drops. Find drops that look like animals.

- **Drip Paint** - Get an appliance box. Cut the large sides off of the box. Put newspaper on the floor by an open wall. Lean one or two of the pieces of cardboard against the wall. Pour tempera paint into small containers with a brush in each one.

  Have a child pick up a tub of paint in one hand, dip the brush into the paint, press it against the cardboard near the top, and watch what happens to the paint. Repeat as often as each child would like.
  Encourage The Children: Find long/short drips, matching color drips, fat/skinny drips, and so on.

- **Roll Out and Paint** - Have one or two rolls of light-colored plain shelf paper, tempera paint, and several types of brushes. Tape one end of the paper to the floor in an open area.

  Have a child begin to roll out the paper and paint. As other children choose to paint, continue to roll the paper out. After everyone has painted, hang it up. "How long is it?"

- **Brush Selection** - Tape a long piece of butcher paper to the table/floor. Pour different colors of paint into shallow containers. Put several different brushes into each paint container. Encourage the children to use the different brushes as they paint.
  Encourage The Children: Find wide/narrow brush strokes. Which brushes do the children think made the different strokes? Why? Which was their favorite brush to paint with?

- **Driving Along** - Tape a piece of butcher paper to the table/floor and pretend that it is the road. Pour tempera paint into shallow containers. Collect a variety of small toy cars, trucks, and scooters.

    Have the children roll a vehicle back and forth in the paint to get the tires full of color. Drive it along the road. Get more paint and continue.
    Encourage The Children: Figure out which vehicles made which tracks?

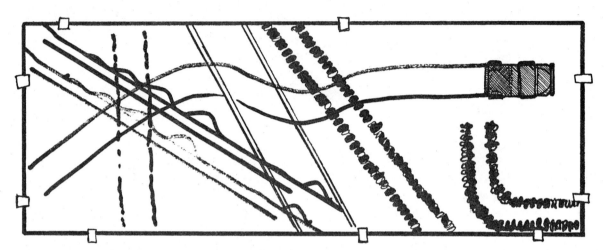

- **Rolling Along** - Tape a long piece of brown mailing paper to the table/floor. Pour bright colored paints into shallow containers. Have 7-8 furniture casters in a container.

    Roll the castor in the paint and then onto the paper. Get more paint and roll again.
    Encourage The Children: Look at all of the different lines, curves, and circles. Are they wide? Narrow?

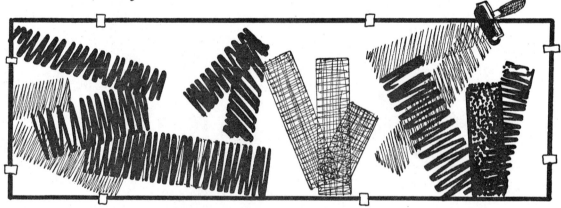

- **Brayer Fun** - Tape a long piece of butcher paper to the table/floor. Pour paint into shallow containers. Put several different size brayers into each container.

    Roll the brayer back and forth in the paint and then onto the paper. Roll more paint using different brayers or other colors.

USING PRINT-MAKING TOOLS

- **One Color Design** - Thoroughly clean the insides of a pumpkin. Cut the rind into pieces. Pour orange paint into several shallow containers. Add the pumpkin pieces to each container. Tape a long sheet of brown mailing paper to the table/floor.

  Dip the pumpkin rind into the paint and print various orange shapes on the paper.

  Encourage The Children: "Kesha, does the shape remind you of something else? What?" Do any children arrange their printing into a particular design? Let a child tell you about it.

- **Kitchen Tool Design** - Gather a variety of kitchen utensils, such as a potato masher, slotted spoon, apple cutter, biscuit cutter, etc. Pour paint into shallow containers. Drape a white sheet over a large table.

  Dip the different tools into the paint and make a colorfully decorated sheet. Let dry and use it as a backdrop, wall decoration, or tablecloth for a parent open house.

  Encourage The Children: Notice all of the designs and shapes as children print.

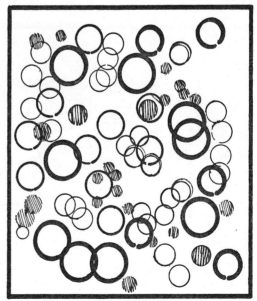

- **Shape Design** - Gather a variety of printing items which are the same shape. For example, collect jar lids, corks, paper cups, spools, and egg carton sections for circles or berry baskets, blocks, square sponges, thick square styrofoam pieces, cardboard dairy containers for squares and so on. Pour paint into shallow containers and tape a long sheet of newsprint on the table/floor.

  Dip the shapes into the paint and make lots of different size circles, squares, or other shape.

USING OTHER TOOLS

- **Straw Paint** - Tape a long piece of white butcher paper to the floor or table. Put lots of different length and width plastic straws in a tray. Have small tubs of paint with a spoon in each one set around the paper. Set a waste container close by.

    Have each child spoon paint onto the paper, choose a straw, and blow the paint around. When finished with each straw, throw it away. Encourage children to use different colors of paint and different size straws.

    Encourage The Children: "Is it hard to blow the paint around?" "What type of straw works best for you?" "Krystal, did any of your colors blend together? Show me!"

- **Drizzle Paint** - Tape a long piece of wallpaper with the non-design side up to the table or floor. (If the wallpaper is narrow tape several strips.) Mix a little liquid starch or white glue to each paint to make it thicker. Pour different colors of thickened tempera paint into plastic mustard and/or ketchup containers.

    Have the children squeeze paint designs all over the paper. When **dry** encourage the children to feel the different lines.

    Encourage The Children: Look for curved, circular, wiggly, straight, and jagged lines.

SMALL PAINT MURALS: Several days after children have painted one of the giant murals, give them the same art materials with much smaller or individual size paper.

Encourage The Children: "B.J., how do you like straw painting on smaller sheets of paper?" "Is it different to drip paint on a small piece of cardboard rather than on a huge one?"

FINGERPAINT MIX AND MATCH: Offer fingerpaints on various papers and surfaces. Have water and paper towels handy for children to easily wash their hands.

- Premixed fingerpaint on large plastic trays or directly on top of the art table.

- Premixed fingerpaint on freezer wrap paper. Paint on the shiny side, let dry overnight, turn over and fingerpaint on the other side.
  Encourage The Children: *"Which side do you like to fingerpaint on the best? Why?"*

- Mud on rubber shower mats. Put mud in large containers. Children can scoop some onto their mats and fingerpaint.
  Encourage The Children: *"How does mud feel?" "How does the mat feel?" "Do you like fingerpainting on it?"*

- Mix flour and water into a fingerpaint consistency. Add cinnamon for a great smell. Fingerpaint on cookie sheets.

FINGERPAINT COLOR MIX: Let the children begin fingerpainting with one color on individual plastic trays. After awhile ask each child if he would like to add a second color. If yes, scoop some additional paint on his tray. (Try these colors in the beginning and then experiment as the children would like - yellow and a little red; green and a little red; yellow and a little blue; red and a little blue; any color and a little white or vice versa; any color and a little black.)
EXTENSION: After children have had lots of opportunities in mixing two colors, offer them 1, 2, and then 3. Start with these combinations and then experiment - green with a little yellow and blue; red with a little blue and yellow; blue with a little black and orange.
Encourage The Children: *"What is happening to the first color when you add the next color?" Add a little more of a color, what now?*

FINGERPAINT FRIENDS: Spray scented or unscented shaving cream directly on the top of the art table. Encourage the children to fingerpaint with large sweeping motions, short finger movements, knuckles and nails, fast and jerky lines, and so on. Some children might want to make designs, pictures, shapes, letters, etc..
Encourage The Children: *"Sasha, you're writing your name." "Billy, you're drawing lines with your fingernails." "Tony, you and Willie are fingerpainting together."*

WATERCOLOR MIX AND MATCH: Offer water color paints with various paint brushes and other tools on paper or other surfaces in a variety of ways.

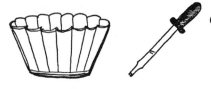

- Colored water and eye droppers on coffee filters.
  Encourage The Children: Watch the drops of colored water as they touch the coffee filters. "What happens?"

- Mix water and food coloring to make lots of colored ice cubes. Wearing mittens, let the children paint manilla paper.

- Watercolors with brushes on wide adding machine paper. As more and more children choose to watercolor, keep rolling the tape out.
  Encourage The Children: Ask the children where they would like to display their colored strip, maybe on their cubbies or around the door.

WET AND WATER COLOR: Use water color tins with brushes on paper plates. Have small containers filled with water to wash brushes off and paper towels to wipe them. Have several larger bowls of water on the art table with wide paint brushes.

Have the children use the wide paint brushes to brush their plates with water. Paint the wet plates with watercolors and small brushes. Remember to wash and wipe the brushes before using a new color. If the plate begins to dry, brush it with more water.

Outside

EASEL PAINTING: Bring your painting easels and supplies outside. After each child has finished his painting, hang it on the fence or from low tree branches with clothespins.

FENCE PAINTING: Use your fence as an outside easel. Clip the paper to fence. Have paint containers in soda cartons so they don't tip.

SNOW PAINTING: Go outside and paint on snow with water color or tempera paints.
EXTENSION: Build a snowman and paint his features.

BUMPY FINGERPAINT: Use fingerpaint paper and different colors of fingerpaint on the blacktop or concrete.
Encourage The Children: *"How does it feel to fingerpaint on the ground rather than on the table?"*

OVERSIZE PAINTINGS: Offer painting activities which take more space.

- **Flick Painting** - Have any type of paper, paints, and easel brushes. Lay the paper on the ground. Dip the brush into the paint and "flick" it at the paper. The paint will fly off the brush. Dip and flick as often as you'd like.

- **Spray Bottle Painting** - Fill 6 or 7 spray bottles about half full of different colors of water. Lay paper on the ground. Spray the paper with all of the colors. Let it dry in the sun.
  Encourage The Children: *Look at the paper after it is dry. How is it different than the paper the children began with?*

- **Big Brush Painting** - Have large sheets of paper, paint poured into large containers, and a variety of large brushes and other tools such as wide paint brushes, scrub brushes, feather dusters, shoe shine brushes, and tree branches.
  Lay the paper on the ground along with the paint and brushes. Choose the brushes/tools and fill the paper with strokes of color.

Crayon
Supply List

Crayons

Erasable
Fabric
Fluorescent
Metallic
Multi-colored
Oil Pastels
Pastels
Regular
Soap
Washable
Water

Shapes

Chubby
Cookie
Sticks
   Circular
   Non-roll (one side flat)
   Hexagon

Sizes

Jumbo
Large
Regular

Crayon On

Fabric
Paper (See Pg. 10)
Plastic Trays
Plates
Sheets
Table Tops
Trays
Warming Trays With
   Paper
Wood

Accessories

Crayon Sharpeners
Vegetable Peelers

Clean-Up

Broom
Dust Pan
Paper Towels
Scouring Pads
Soap
Sponges
Water

Recipes

Multi-Colored Crayons

<u>You'll Need:</u>
Non-stick muffin pans
Old crayons

<u>To Make:</u> Peel the paper off of the crayons. Put 5-10 crayon pieces in each muffin space. Pre-heat your oven to 250°. Put the muffin pan/s into the oven. Let the crayons melt. Turn off the oven. Leave the pan in the oven until the crayons have hardened (overnight). Pull out the muffin pan and pop out the crayons.

Soap Crayons

<u>You'll Need:</u>
Soap Flakes
Water
Food Coloring

<u>To Make:</u> Measure 1/8 cup of water and add food coloring to make vivid colors. Pour the colored liquid into a bowl. Add 7/8 cup of soap flakes. Mix well. Press the mixture into sections of an ice cube tray. Let it set in a warm place for several days. Pop the crayons out.

Sun Crayons

<u>You'll Need:</u>
Egg Cartons or Disposal Cups
Old Crayons

<u>To Make:</u> Peel the paper off of the crayons. Break the crayons into small pieces. Put several pieces into each egg cup or disposable cup. Put the cups on a tray and set the tray in the hot sun. Let the crayons melt. Leave them out overnight to harden. Pop your new crayons out of their containers.

At The Easel

EASEL MIX AND MATCH: Offer various crayons with all types of paper.

- Jumbo crayons on the backside of large wallpaper samples.

- Multi-colored crayons on pizza boards.
  Encourage The Children: Say, "Look Ericka, you are using round crayons and round paper."

- Fluorescent crayons on paper grocery bags.

- Regular crayons on strips of adding machine tape.

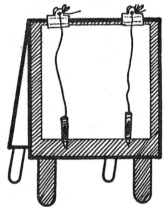

TWO FISTED COLORING: Using long pieces of yarn, hang a jumbo/large crayon on each side of the easel board, from long pieces of yarn. Use regular easel paper. Let the children color with both crayons at the same time. They might want to crayon with both hands or put two crayons in one hand and color.
Encourage The Children: You could say, "How do you like coloring with both hands?"

CRAYON CLUMPS: Group regular size crayons with paper on them into piles of 3 or 4 each. Tape each group together with masking tape. Put several 'crayon clumps' in each easel tray. Crayon on white paper.
Encourage The Children: Talk with them about the different colors in their 'clumps.' Ask a child, "Are you drawing with all of the colors in your clump or are you using certain colors?"

EASEL RUBBINGS: First make 'shape papers.' Get 5-10 pieces of easel paper. From construction paper cut out a variety of large geometric shapes. Glue several (3-5) shapes on each piece of easel paper. Have them ready for children to choose from.

Put crayons with the paper peeled off in the easel tray. Let a child choose a 'shape paper' and clip it to the easel. Then clip a piece of blank easel paper over the 'shape paper' and let the child make rubbings of the shapes.

On The Table/Floor

CRAYON MIX AND MATCH: Offer a variety of crayons on papers and other surfaces.

- Soap crayons on the top of the art table or on large plastic trays. Remember, washing the trays or table is a great part of this activity.

- Fabric crayons on T-shirts. (Then go on a picnic or have a celebration so that everyone can wear their newly colored shirts.)

- Multi-colored crayons on the backside of wallpaper.
  Encourage The Children: "Turn your crayon and make a line. What colors appeared?" "Tell me about your picture." "Do you like to use these crayons? Why/why not?"

TABLETOP RUBBINGS: Crayons with the paper peeled off, different textures taped to the tabletop, and a long piece of blank paper over the textures.

- Using posterboard, cut out lots of large geometric shapes, toy shapes, vegetable/fruit shapes, clothes shapes, different size raindrops, and so on. Tape one set of shapes to a large table. Cover it with newsprint. Have the children rub their hands over the paper to find the different shapes and then make rubbings of them with crayons.

- Different wall paneling samples covered with butcher paper.

- Textured wallpaper pieces covered with newsprint.

- Variety of leaves from your locale covered with light colored butcher paper. Maybe the leaves could be collected by the children on a 'leaf hunt' before the activity.

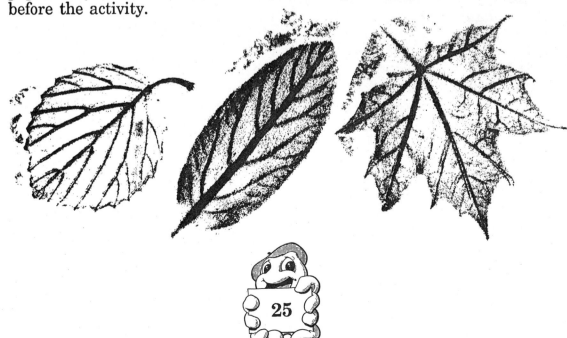

CRAYON HUNTS: Hide crayons around the room before the children arrive. Set up different activities in which children look for and find the crayons, and then do an activity with them.

- Hide only red crayons. Find and bring them to the art table, and use them to color on a piece of pink butcher paper.

Say to the children, *"Someone hid all of our crayons last night. He left us a note. It says, 'I hid your crayons all around the room. Find them and put them in the empty crayon basket on the art table. Have fun coloring pictures on the manilla paper.'"*

- Hide only crayons with the paper peeled off. Find them. Using typing paper, have the children to make rubbings of different things in the classroom -- walls, floor, tile, blocks, door, etc.

- Hide all of the crayons. Find them and use them to color plain paper placemats on the warming tray. (Remember safety.)

ARM DANCING: Have the children kneel/sit on the floor around a long piece of mural paper. Put a variety of different crayons in a container. Let each child choose 2 crayons and hold one in each hand. Begin playing music.

Tell the children to let their arms dance around the paper, coloring as they move. Change to another type of music -- dance again.
Encourage The Children: *Hang the mural low on a wall or bulletin board. Talk about the different types of crayon strokes. "Can you tell which crayon strokes were drawn to the different types of music? How?" "Find strokes you think were made with jumbo crayons." Multi-colored crayons, fluorescent, etc.*

26

CRAYON MELT: Have the children use the sun to melt crayons and then use them in a variety of activities.

- Using pencil/crayon sharpeners and old crayons make shavings. Before going outside, sprinkle shavings on small pieces of construction paper (4½"x6"). Carry the art outside and lay it on the ground in the sun. Watch what happens to the crayon shavings. When you go back inside, carry the art back. Watch what happens to the melted crayons.

- Break up old crayons and put them in aluminum foil cupcake liners. Take them outside along with old toothbrushes and paper. Put the crayons in the sun. Watch them melt. Use the melted crayons and toothbrushes to 'crayon paint' on paper.

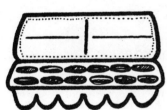

- Make 'multi-colored crayons' using the sun rather than the oven for heat. Break up old crayons and put them in styrofoam egg carton cups. Take the egg carton outside and set it in a secluded, but sunny place. Let the crayons melt. Leave them outside to harden overnight. Early the next morning, bring them inside and pop them out of the egg cups. Use the new crayons to color a giant mural.

OUTSIDE RUBBINGS: Cut pieces of typing paper into quarters. Put them in a pile along with crayons which have the papers peeled off. Encourage the children to walk around and make rubbings of different textures outside. At the bottom of each one, write what the rubbing was taken from. After all of the rubbings have been made, glue them to a large piece of colored butcher paper and display them for everyone to see.

VARIATION: Lay a long piece of white butcher paper on the concrete/blacktop. Secure it with bricks. Using the sides of crayons, have the children make a giant rubbing of their playground surface.

Encourage The Children: *"Show me your rubbings." "What surfaces did you use?" "Look carefully at the rubbing of the playground you made. Is it the same all over the paper?"*

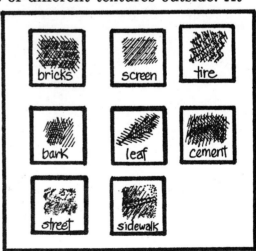

Paste/Glue
Supply List

Paste/Glue

Flour/Water Paste
Glue Stick
Library Paste
Liquid Starch
School Glue
Wheat Paste
White Glue
White Paste

Accessories

Collage Box
Scissors
Small Brushes
Small Squeeze Bottles

Paste/Glue On

Boxes (All Types and
   Sizes)
Carpet Tubes
Giant Greeting Cards
Packing Peanuts
Paper (See Pg. 10)
Paper Towel Rolls
Plastic Placemats
Plastic Trays
Plates
Pizza Boards
Posters
Table Top
Trays
Wrapping Paper Tubes

Clean-Up

Paper Towels
Soap
Sponges
Water

Collage Materials *

Aluminum Foil

Apple Seeds

Bark

Beads

Beans

Bias Tape

Bottle Caps

Boxes

Braiding

Buttons

Cardboard Tubes

Carpet Pieces

Confetti

Cord

Corks

Cotton Balls and Batting

Cupcake Liners

Dried Flowers

Easter Grass

Egg Carton Pieces

Fabrics (All Types)

Feathers

Foam Pieces

Jar Lids

Lace

Meat Trays

Nature Items

Nut Cups

Paper (See Pg. 10)

Pastas

Pipe Cleaners

Popsicle Sticks

Ribbons

Rope

Rubber Bands

Sticks

Spools

String

Stones

Straws

Styrofoam

Tape (All Types)

Tiles

Tongue Depressors

Twine

Wires

Wood Pieces

Yarn

* or any other materials you may have around

Recipes

FLOUR/WATER PASTE

You'll Need:
Flour
Water

To Make: Pour 1 cup of flour into a large bowl. Slowly add 1¼ cups of water, stirring all of the time. The paste should be a creamy consistency. Add more flour or water if necessary.

Get the supplies

Pour in the flour

Add water and stir

Mix until creamy

PASTE FINGERPAINT: Offer different types of paste on a variety of surfaces. Have water and paper towels nearby so that children can wash their hands.

- Flour/water paste on plastic trays. You can mix the paste with the children and then let them fingerpaint with it.
  Encourage The Children: *"Jackie, how does the paste feel?" "Hold up your hands. What do you see?" "Ortiz, is the paste smooth? Sticky? Slippery? Watery?"*

- White paste on the table top. Have a spray bottle with a little water in it to keep the paste slightly moist.

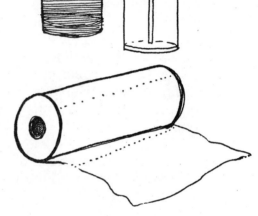

- Library paste on a plastic carpet protector strip.
  Encourage The Children: *"How does the paste feel?" "Do your fingers feel the bumps in the plastic.*

- Liquid starch on plastic placemats.
  Encourage The Children: *"Does the starch look like paste?" "How does the starch feel on your fingers?" "Smell the starch. Tell me about it."*

- White paste on cookie sheets. Add several drops of green food coloring (any color/s) to the paste for children to work in.
  Encourage The Children: *"What color paste are you mixing?" "Look at your fingers. What color is on them?"*

TWO-DIMENSIONAL COLLAGES: Offer a variety of two-dimensional collage materials on different papers. When organizing your collage materials, have a divided box, a lazy susan tray, or another way of keeping the materials separated and neat, so that the children can easily see and work with all of the materials.

- Variety of red or any color papers and ribbons on white construction paper with red colored paste. (Add red food coloring to paste and mix.) *Encourage The Children: Have the children name all of the collage materials. Have them look around the room and find other red things. Ask a child, "Cliff, are you wearing anything that is red? Point to it."*

- A variety of papers cut into different size circles on round paper plates or on posterboard cut into circles with white glue. VARIATION: One type and color of paper, such as blue construction paper cut into many different size triangles on pennant shaped paper.

- Different length strips of colored paper on a long sheet of narrow white shelf paper with glue sticks.
Encourage The Children: Have the children find the longest/shortest strips and widest/narrowest strips. Ask children how they like using a glue stick.

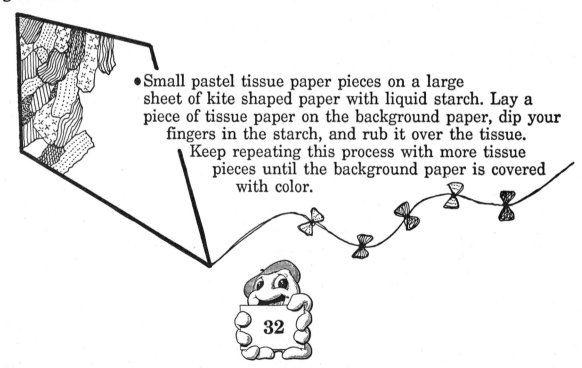

- Small pastel tissue paper pieces on a large sheet of kite shaped paper with liquid starch. Lay a piece of tissue paper on the background paper, dip your fingers in the starch, and rub it over the tissue. Keep repeating this process with more tissue pieces until the background paper is covered with color.

32

THREE-DIMENSIONAL COLLAGES: Offer a variety of three-dimensional collage materials on different papers and surfaces with pastes/glues.

- Leaves and other nature objects, which the children collected while on a nature walk, on paper grocery bags with white glue.

- Round objects on a large pizza board with glue.

- Bottle caps on brown mailing paper with glue.

- Small containers (cupcake liners, egg carton sections, candy liners, berry baskets, plastic food dividers) on cardboard with glue.

- Small wooden objects (spools, toothpicks, wood scraps, clothespins, bark, small twigs, pencils, popsicle sticks, dowel rod pieces) on a thin piece of plywood with brown colored glue.

wood collage box

BOX CONSTRUCTION: Offer a variety of all sizes and types of cardboard tubes, cartons, and boxes with white glue and brushes.

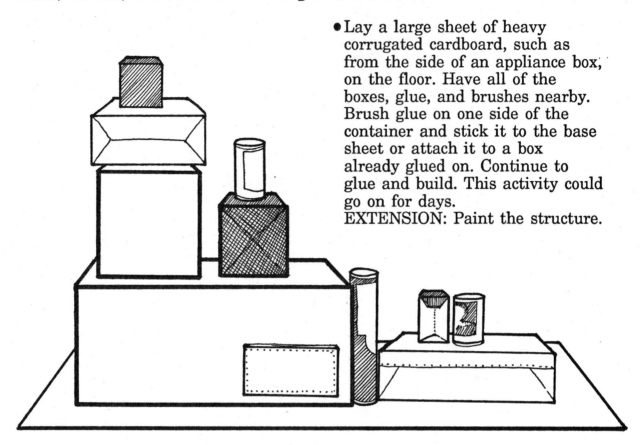

- Lay a large sheet of heavy corrugated cardboard, such as from the side of an appliance box, on the floor. Have all of the boxes, glue, and brushes nearby. Brush glue on one side of the container and stick it to the base sheet or attach it to a box already glued on. Continue to glue and build. This activity could go on for days.
  EXTENSION: Paint the structure.

- Have a very large box, other smaller boxes, cartons, and tubes, glue and brushes. Put the activity in a quiet area. On the first day have the children glue smaller containers to the topside of the large box. Let it dry overnight. On the next day turn the box. Glue more containers to the new topside. Continue until 5 of the 6 sides have been added to.
  EXTENSION: Have the children dictate a story to you about their structure. Write it down. Mount the story on a piece of construction paper and display it with the structure.

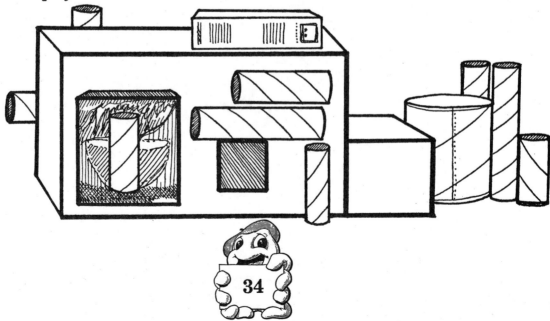

34

GLUE MOBILES: Cut pieces of yarn, string, ribbon, and/or twine. Lay them neatly on a placemat and set in the middle of your outside table. Mix a little water into white glue so that it is thinned down. Pour this 'thinned down' glue into several small margarine tubs. Keep them covered when not in use so that the glue does not dry up in the sun.

- Give a child a piece of waxed paper and set it on the table. Have him dip a piece of yarn into the glue, pull it out, pinch it at the top between his thumb and index finger, and slide his fingers down the yarn removing the excess glue. Lay the sticky yarn on the piece of waxed paper. Have him continue making more sticky yarn pieces and laying them on top of each other in any design he chooses.

  Bring the mobiles inside and let them dry overnight. After they are dry, tie another piece of yarn to each one for hanging. VARIATION: Repeat this process on other days with different types of yarn and other 'strings' that you have access to.

- Have children work together on this mobile. Blow up a small balloon. As above, dip yarn or other strings into 'thinned down' glue. Have one child gently hold the balloon and another child drape sticky yarn pieces around it. Trade jobs every once in awhile. Hang the balloons from a tree or on the fence to dry. After each one is dry, remove the balloon and hang the mobile inside or outside.

Scissors
Supply List

Scissors

Beginner Squeeze-Type
Cushion Grip (left/right)
Paper Only
Safety
Training

Cut

Boxes
Coffee Stir Sticks
Cord
Corrugated Strips
Crepe Paper
Cupcake Liners
Egg Cartons
Elastic Tape
Fabrics
Magazines
Packing Peanuts
Paper (See Pg. 10)
Pipe Cleaners
Ribbon
Rubber Bands
Straws
String
Twine
Yarn

HANDY HINT:

OPEN SHUT: As children cut, have them say "Open-Shut" to themselves.

Accessories

Collage Box
Glue
Lazy Susan Tray
Paper Punch
Paste
Scissors Rack
Tape

Clean-Up

Broom
Dust Pan
Scissors Rack

SNIPPING MIX AND MATCH: Offer a variety of papers which are easy to cut with one 'snip' of the scissors.

- Tape a variety of long, narrow strips of paper to the art table. Have a sandwich bag for each child with his name on it. Let each child 'snip' as many pieces as he would like off the ends of the strips, and put them in his bag to take home.

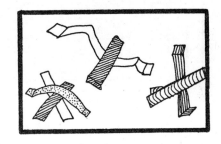

Encourage The Children: As children are snipping, have them chant to themselves, "open-shut" as they snip pieces of paper. This will help them get the rhythm of cutting.

- Cut a variety of different papers into varying length and width strips. Put them in a collage box. Have each child choose strips he would like, snip them into lengths he would like, and put them on a meat tray. He can then display his strips by pasting them onto a piece of paper.

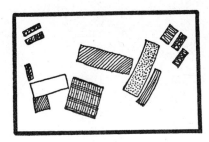

- Roll up different colors of duplicating paper into tubes. Put a rubber band around each tube to hold it on place. Store the tubes for several days so that the paper naturally curls. Put the tubes on the art table. Have children 'snip, snip, snip' the ends of the tubes to get curly-cues. Glue one end of each curly-cue to a big piece of butcher paper. Display the 'colored curly-cues' on your door.

- Cut different colors of construction paper into 1"x12" strips. With a marker draw a line at the 6" place on each strip. Let the children cut the strips in half by making 'snips' on the lines. Put the strips on a tray.

  Help the children use the strips which they have cut to make an easy, colorful, 'raindrop chain' for the classroom.

37

FRINGING MIX AND MATCH: Offer a variety of paper strips which the children can fringe with scissors. Tape the top, long side of each strip to your art table/floor. Have children cut to the tape along the entire strip. Use the fringe to border bulletin boards, doors, windows, etc.

- Long strips of adding machine paper with paper punches. First let the children punch lots of holes in the paper and then fringe it with scissors.

- Crepe paper streamers with scissors.
  Encourage The Children: *"Is cutting the crepe paper different from other paper that you've cut?" "Having trouble cutting this paper? Try going a little slower."*

- Colored butcher paper with scissors.

CUTTING MIX AND MATCH: Offer children a wide variety of papers and other surfaces to cut. Have a special place for the children to put the pieces they have cut. For example have labeled meat trays on the table. Or you can

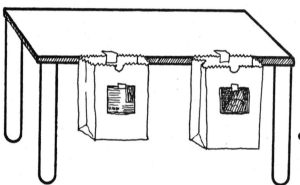

get lunch size paper bags. Label them with the type of paper you want children to put in them. Tape the bag/s to the edge of the art table for easy use. Later put the children's cuttings into the collage box for pasting and gluing.

- Find and cut out happy and sad pictures from magazine pages. Put them on labeled meat trays.

- Cut large scrap pieces of colored construction paper into smaller pieces. Put the pieces into bags marked by color.

- Cut wallpaper samples. Sort the cuttings into bags marked by design.

- Cut (tear) tissue paper. Put these pieces on separate meat trays.

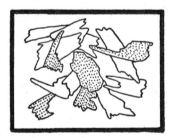 

- Cut old greeting cards and colored ribbons. Put them into bags marked for cards and ribbons.

- Cut cardboard containers such as cereals, eggs, cake mixes, etc. Sort them into bags marked for flat pieces, chunks, and bits.

CUT AND STOP: Offer the children a variety of long pieces of paper to cut on. Using a marker, draw various types of vertical lines on the papers spaced far enough apart so that children have room to cut. Tape each 'cut and stop' paper to an empty wall at a height which the children can easily use.

- Shelf paper with wide straight lines going to the tape.

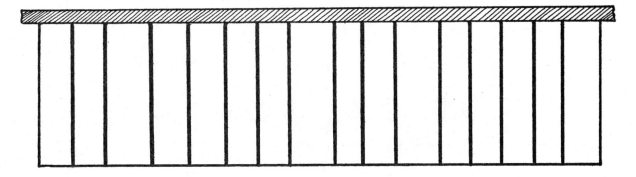

- Butcher paper with wide straight lines stopping at different lengths.

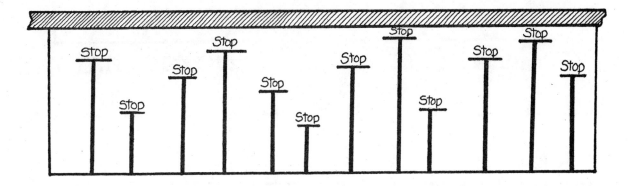

- Brown mailing paper with wide varying lines stopping at the tape.

CUTTING CARDS: Using construction paper or wallpaper, make a variety of individual 'cutting cards' which children can use for cutting. Put the cards on the shelf for easy access. Put the cuttings on trays and later into the collage box for paste/glue activities.

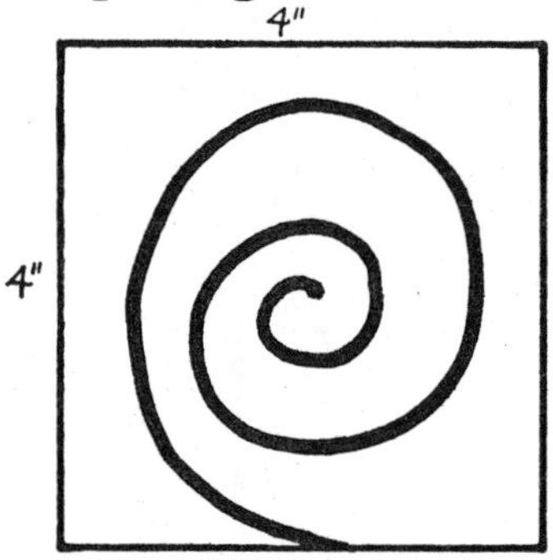

4"
4"

Curl It Card

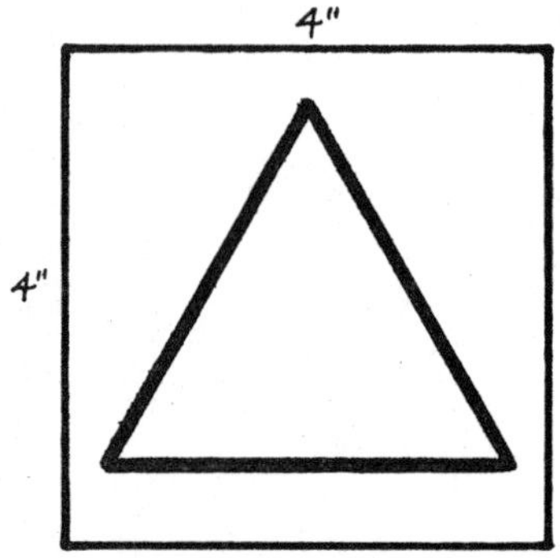

4"
4"

Shape Card

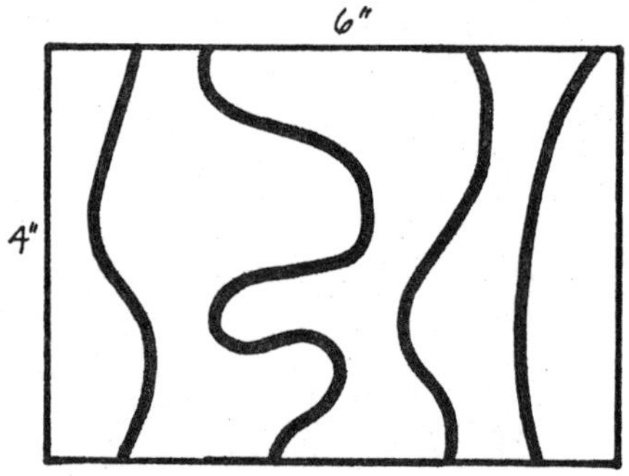

6"
4"

Curved Card

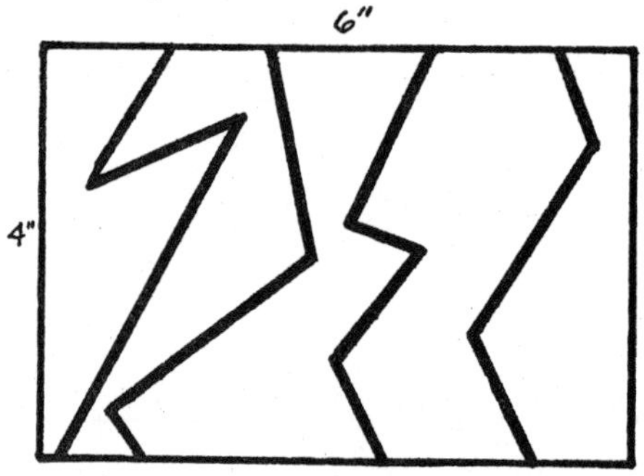

6"
4"

Zig-Zag Card

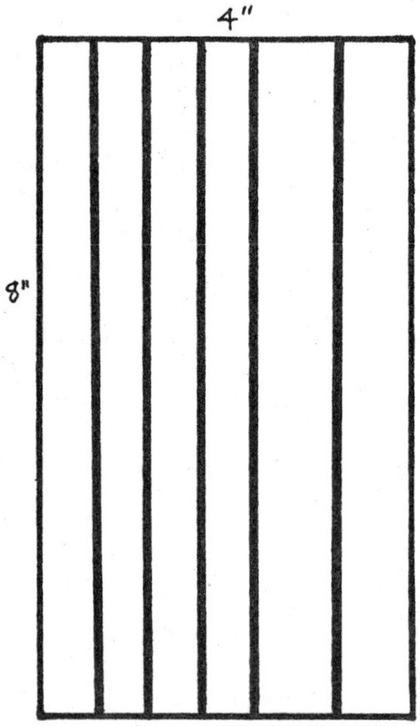

4"
8"

Strip Card

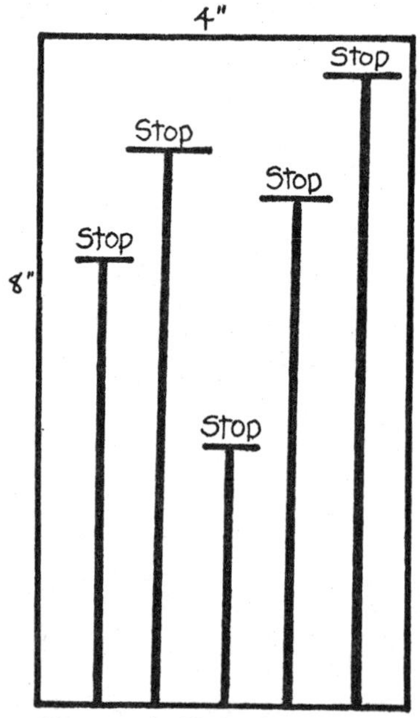

4"
Stop
Stop
Stop
Stop
Stop
8"

Cut & Stop Card

4"
8"

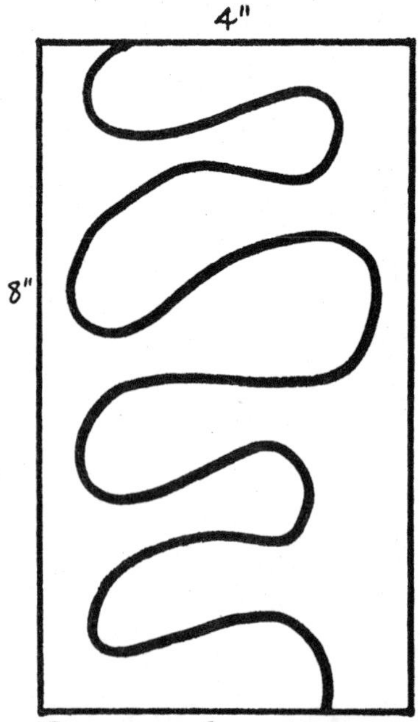

Squiggley Card

Outside

YARD SCULPTURE: Take different colors and types of yarn outside. Have the children cut different length pieces off of the skeins. Place the yarn pieces over tree branches, around bushes, along the edges of your sand area, end to end for a maze, and other places in your outdoor space.

VARIATION: Get small tree branches. Cut yarn pieces and weave them in, out, around, and through the branches. You might stand the branches in flower pots for decoration around the yard.

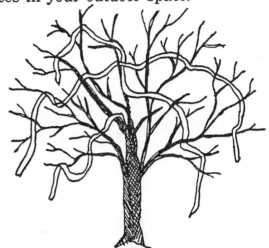

Encourage The Children: *"Greg, what color yarn are you hanging over the branch?" "You're putting a short yellow piece on the bush." "Eric, go get a green piece of yarn and I'll help you start weaving."*

FENCE WEAVING: Cut colored butcher paper or fabric into 3'x2" strips. Clip the strips to your fence with clothespins. Tie several pairs of scissors onto the fence near the strips. Have the children 'snip' pieces from the strips and then weave them through the holes/openings in the fence. You might have extra clothespins available for the children to use to secure one end of their strips while weaving.

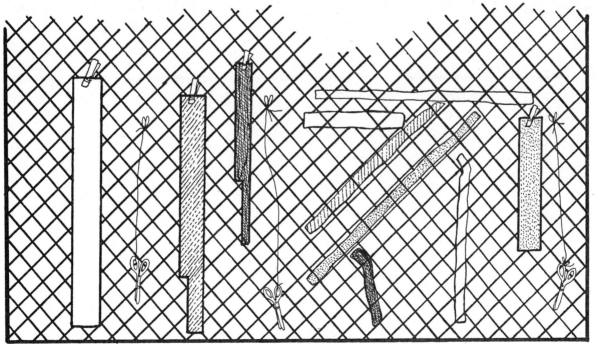

Dough
Supply List

Doughs

Cloud Dough
Sawdust Dough
Silly Putty
Soap Dough
Soft Dough

Dough On

Aluminum Foil Pan
Bread Board
Brownie Pan
Carpet Protector Strip
Cookie Sheet
Desk/Chair Floor Protector
Formica
Freezer Paper
Glossy Wallpaper
Linoleum Pieces
Masonite Pieces
Oilcloth
Pegboard Pieces
Pie Pan
Plastic Placemat
Rubber Shower Mat
Tabletop
Trays

Add 'Coloring'

Food Coloring
Powdered Tempera Paint

Add 'Texture'

Beads
Gravel
Kosher Salt
Popcorn Kernels
Sand
Whole Cloves

Add 'Smell'

Cinnamon
Extracts
    Peppermint
    Vanilla
Gelatin
Lemon Juice
Powdered Fruit Drink
    Mixes

Accessories

Blunt Table Knives
Blunt Pencils
Blunt Scissors
Bobby Pins
Bottle Caps
Candles
Chop Sticks
Clothespins
Coffee Stir Sticks
Combs
Cookie Cutters
Craft Sticks
Dowel Rods
Film Canisters
Forks
Ice Cream Spoons
Jar Lids
Measuring Cups
Paper Towel Rolls
Ping-Pong Balls
Pipe Cleaners
Plastic Blocks
Plastic Containers
Plastic Flower Pots
Plastic Straws
Popsicle Sticks
Potato Masher
Rolling Pins
Spray Can Lids
Telephone Wire
Toilet Paper Rolls
Toothpicks
Twigs
Wooden Blocks
Wooden Spools

HANDY HINT:

MOISTEN-UP: If your dough begins to dry up, add a little liquid to it. Put it in an airtight container and let it set in the refrigerator.

Clean-Up

Broom
Dull Plastic Knives
Dust Pan
Paper Towels
Sponges

Soft Dough

<u>You'll Need:</u>

5 cups of flour
1 cup salt
4T alum
2T vegetable oil
3 cups water
Food coloring (optional)

<u>To Make</u>: Boil the water. Add food coloring to the water if you want a colored dough. Mix all of the dry ingredients in a large bowl. Add the boiling water. Stir together. When the mixture is cool enough, put it on the table and knead it until it is thoroughly mixed.

<u>To Store</u>: Put the dough in a tightly covered container. Keep it in the refrigerator overnight. If the dough begins to get dry, add a little water.

Cloud Dough

<u>You'll Need:</u>

1 cup vegetable oil
6 cups flour
1 cup water
Food coloring (optional)

<u>To Make</u>: Add your food coloring to the water. Put the flour and oil into a large bowl. Slowly add the water, stirring as you pour. Continue mixing the ingredients until you get a soft dough. Add a little more water or flour if necessary. Put the dough on the table and knead it until it is completely blended. This dough will be have an oily texture.

<u>To Store</u>: Put the dough in a covered plastic container or a plastic bag.

Sawdust Dough

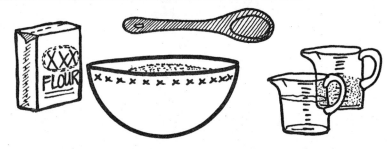

You'll Need:

2 cups flour
4 cups sawdust
2 cups water

To Make: Put the dry ingredients in a large bowl. Slowly add the water and mix thoroughly. Continue stirring until the mixture forms a soft, textured dough. Add more water if necessary. Put the dough on the table and knead it until it is completely blended.

To Store: Put the dough in a tightly covered container and keep it in the refrigerator overnight. Add a little water to it each morning.

Silly Putty

You'll Need:

2/3 cup white glue
1/3 cup liquid starch (Sta-Flo)

To Make: Pour both ingredients in a large bowl. Mix them together using a heavy-duty spoon or hand mixer. If you have a little liquid left, pour it off.

To Store: Put the dough in a tightly covered container or plastic bag. It will be a little stiff each morning so knead it until it softens up.

Soap Dough

You'll Need:

4 cups of soap flakes
1 cup water
Food coloring (optional)

To Make: Put the soap flakes in a large bowl. Add the food coloring to the water. Slowly pour the water into the soap flakes, stirring while pouring. Keep stirring until the ingredients are well mixed.

To Store: This dough only lasts one day. If a child molds something, set it on a paper plate to firm up overnight.

DOUGH MIX AND MATCH: Offer doughs on different surfaces without any accessories.

- Soft dough on the art table. Have the children use their hands, fingers, knuckles, nails, palms, wrists, etc.
  Encourage The Children: "Tracey, you're making finger holes in your dough." "Can you make your balls of dough really flat like a pancake? Can I watch you?" "Let's make thumb prints in your dough." "Who's got the biggest print?"

- Soft dough on rubber shower mats.
  Encourage The Children: "Do you feel the bumpy mat as you're playing with the dough?"

- Soap dough on styrofoam plates. If children have molded something, let it sit out overnight and it will harden. Carefully put it in a sandwich bag for the child to take home.

- Sawdust dough on a bread board.
  Encourage The Children: Tell the children where you got the sawdust to make the dough. Ask them if anyone they know builds with wood. "What do they build?"

- Silly putty on the art table.
  Encourage The Children: "Let's pull the putty." "Is it going to break?"

DRAMATIC PLAY: Use any of the doughs with specific accessories on the art table to encourage pretending. Have special headbands which the children can wear while playing.

- Soft dough with birthday candles, small plates, and blunt knives.

- Sawdust dough with wooden hammers, golf tees, and blunt knives.

- Soft dough, rolling pins, bread boards, cookie cutters, large serving plate, and small plates.

MAKING DOUGH: Choose a dough recipe, get the supplies, and make it with your children on the art table.
EXTENSION: Duplicate the 'dough chart' and glue it to a piece of construction paper. Let the children follow the pictures as they help you make the dough.

Get the supplies

Pour dry ingredients

Pour the water

Mix the ingredients

Knead the dough

Play with the dough

TEXTURED DOUGH: Have a small container of whole cloves. As the children begin to use the dough, have them knead the cloves into it. When you make new batches of dough add different textures.
Encourage The Children: "Mamood, is it hard to hide all of the cloves in your dough?" "Rich, when you're poking the dough do the cloves stick you?" "Do they hurt?"

PINCH AND POKE: Any dough on the art table. As the children are molding their dough, encourage them to roll, punch, poke, pinch, flatten, stretch, squeeze, and manipulate it as many ways as they can think of.
Encourage The Children: "Wow, your dough is long! What are you doing?" "You're rolling your dough." "Are you making something?" "Ricky, your dough is so flat. It almost looks like a pancake."

DOUGH SHAPES: Soft dough on the art table. Have the children roll their pieces of dough into long 'snakes' and then use it to form letters, shapes, squiggles, designs, and so on. You might offer a blunt knife to cut the dough into pieces.

DOUGH ADDITIONS: Use any of the doughs with a variety of accessories.

- Silly putty on the art table with blunt table knives.
  Encourage The Children: "Do you use knives when you eat?" "What foods do you cut with knives?"

- Soft dough on large wooden trays with all types of wooden accessories such as rolling pins, popsicle sticks, mallets, clothespins, toothpicks, etc.
  EXTENSION: Another time offer dough on large plastic trays with several plastic accessories such as coffee stir sticks, combs, cookie cutters, measuring cups, straws, and so on.
  Offer dough on the art table with several metal accessories.

- Sawdust or soft dough with rolling pins on textured mats and trays such as pegboard pieces, pie pans with holes in the bottom, plastic placemats, or rubber shower mats. Have the children roll pieces of dough onto the textured surface. Then carefully lift up the dough and look at the bottom of the dough.
  Encourage The Children: "Mary, what does the bottom of the dough look like?" "Feel the texture." "Does the design on the dough look like the pie pan?"

Outside

INTRODUCE PLASTICINE: Plasticine is a soft, manufactured type of clay which is easy to roll, mold, and work with. Bring a table outside and cover it with a piece of oilcloth or have plastic placemats or individual Masonite boards to work on. Give children balls of plasticine and have them to simply work with it as they choose.

Encourage The Children: "Jesse, how does your clay feel?" "What are you going to do with it?" "Let me watch you." "Let's all roll it and see what happens." "Does it smell? Like what?"

INTRODUCE MODELING CLAY: Modeling clay is a little more difficult to manipulate than plasticine. Have plastic trays or placemats available on a table in the shade. When children begin to work with the clay have them 'softened it' by holding it in their hands or leaving it in the warmth of the sun. Once it is pliable, it is much easier to mold, poke, and flatten.

After children have had many opportunities to simply use it as they wish, you can also enjoy activities with the clay.

- You mold a figure such as a red ball and let the children copy you.

- You mold a pattern of colored balls, such as red-green, red-green, and let the children copy the pattern.

- Mold 3-7 'snakes' each one slightly longer than the last one. Let the children put them in order from shortest to longest or longest to shortest.

- Mold a bunch of different sizes and colors of balls. Describe one, such as, "I'm looking for the largest red ball." A child can point to it or take it and then put it in front of him.

- You mold a colored ball. Let a child mold a ball and place it on top of yours. Another child molds a third ball and sets it on top of the tower. See how high you can make your tower. Count the balls as you go. Count all of the 'red' balls or 'blue' ones. When your tower falls, start all over again. Does the next one have more or less balls than the first one?

Marker/Pencil

Supply List

Markers

Fluorescent
Pastel
Scented
Tempera Sponge-Type
Watercolors

Marker On

Masking Tape
Paper (See Pg. 10)
Plastic Placemats
Plates
Trays

Marker Tips

Fine
Jumbo
Regular
Wedge

Marker Clean-Up

Paper Towels
Soap
Sponge
Water

Pencils

Beginner
Carpenter
Colored
Grease
Mechanical
Regular
Variety Color

Pencil Accessories

Erasers
Grips
Rulers
Sharpeners
Stencils
Templates

Pencil On

Aluminum Foil Pans
Oilcloth
Paper (See Pg. 10)
Plates
Trays

Pencil Clean-Up

Broom
Dust Pan
Paper Towels
Sponge
Soap
Water

At The Easel

EASEL MIX AND MATCH: Offer various pencils with all types of paper.

- Grease pencils on freezer wrap paper.
  Encourage The Children: *"Ty, is it hard to draw with this type of pencil?" "Does your drawing smear when you touch it?" "Touch a line. Does it feel sticky?"*

- Carpenter pencils on the backside of wallpaper.
  Encourage The Children: *"Ortiz, have you ever used this kind of pencil before?" "You sure can make different types of lines with your pencil." "Carpenters use these pencils. They often mark their wood with them, so they know where to cut it."*

- Dull, regular pencils on corrugated paper.
  Encourage The Children: *"Was it fun making 'bumpety-bump' lines across your paper?" "Did you make any lines in the valleys? Show me." "Did you make any lines on the tops of the hills? Where?"*

- Beginner pencils on paper bags. Have pencil sharpeners handy.

PENCIL PALS: Make several pairs of 'pencil pal' headbands. Have a variety of pencils in the easel tray. Hang a piece of easel paper. When two children come to the easel they should put on the  headbands. One child makes a line with his pencil, his buddy adds onto the line, and the first child continues it with his pencil. They continue taking turns extending the line all around the paper, until they decide that their design is finished.

PENCIL PACKS: Gather different pencils into groups of 2, 3 or 4 each. Tape each group together with masking tape. Put several 'pencil packs' in the easel tray. Let children scribble, draw, and mark on large white paper.
Encourage The Children: *"How do you hold your 'pencil pack' when you draw?" "Is it different than when you hold one pencil?" "Tell me about all of your different lines."*

On The Table/Floor

MARKER/PENCIL MIX AND MATCH: Offer a variety of pencils and/or markers on paper and other surfaces. Remember that markers sometimes bleed through paper, so protect the surface with newspapers.

- Grease pencils on large plastic trays. Have small cloths available for children to rub their drawings off when finished, so that the tray is ready for another child.

- Colored pencils on adding machine paper. Cut 3 or 4 strips of paper the length of your art table. Tape the ends of each strip to the table. Add more strips as each one becomes filled with color.

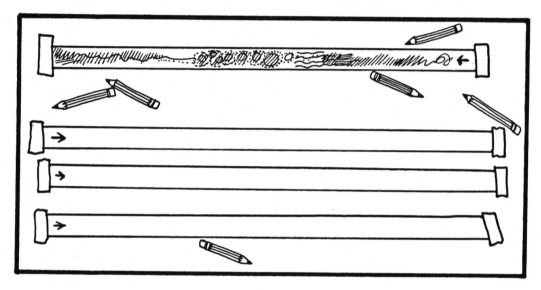

- Fluorescent markers on mailing paper.

- Jumbo markers on newsprint.
  Encourage The Children: *"Is drawing with markers the same as using pencils? Why/why not?"*

- All types of markers, but only one color on butcher paper.

- Jumbo markers on paper towels.
  Encourage The Children: *"Is it hard to draw on paper towels?" "What happens to the ink when you draw on these towels?"*

- Watercolor markers on waxed paper. Hang the drawings in a sunny window.

TEMPLATE DESIGN: Using large, heavy-duty paper or coffee can lids cut a variety of simple, geometric, toy, food, nature, etc. templates that you think that your children would like.

Put the templates on the table along with pencils or narrow markers and light colored paper. Let the children use them as they choose.

Encourage The Children: Show them how to go slowly, pressing against the templates.

DOTS AND LINES: Tempera sponge-type markers and colored pencils on large pieces of light colored butcher paper. Let the children have fun making colored dots and then connecting them with colored pencils.

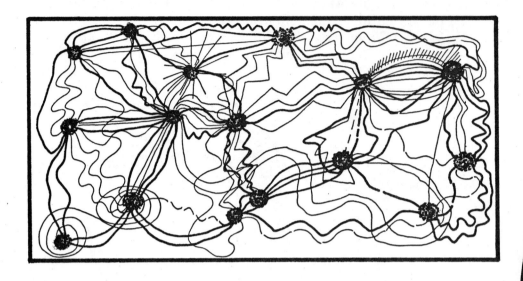

SQUIGGLE AND STRAIGHT: Regular watercolor markers on a long piece of shelf paper. Have children use their markers to make as many different lines, marks, dots, dashes, and curves as they can think of.
Encourage The Children: *"Tell me about the marks you are making." "Which marks do you like to draw the most?" "Look at all of the lines you've made!!"*

COLORFUL STYROFOAM: Unsharpened or very dull beginner pencils, markers, and a large piece of thick styrofoam. Use the pencils to make narrow, wide, shallow, and deep valleys in the styrofoam. Color the styrofoam with the markers. Display it on a window ledge.

Outside

COLORFUL TAPE: Narrow markers on masking tape. Let each child determine how long he wants his tape to be. Cut that length and stick it to an outside table. Let him decorate it with markers. After each child has finished, have him take his tape off of the table and put it on a large piece of newsprint. Write each child's name under his tape. Hang the colorful tape mural on your fence.

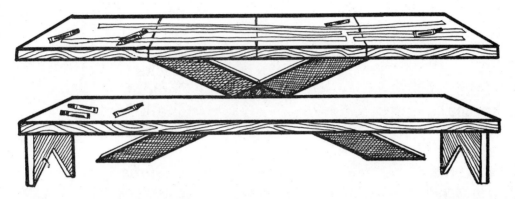

DOODLING AROUND: Markers, pencils, paint, chalk, and crayons on a long piece of white butcher paper. Tape the paper on an outside table. The first day have paint and brushes available. Let the children paint as they wish. The next day let add crayon drawings to their painting. Next time add markers, then pencils, and finally chalk.

BODY TRACINGS:
Beginner pencils, jumbo markers, and butcher paper. Cut butcher paper into pieces the height of your children. Have a child lie on the paper and then trace around him with the heavy pencil. Help him carry his tracing to a shady area where he can add detail and color with the markers. Continue with other children who'd like to make tracings.

Chalk

Supply List

Chalk

Chalkboard
   White
   Colored
Charcoal
Drawing
   Charcoal Sticks
   Colored
   Pastels
Poster

Chalk On

Blacktop
Bricks
Cement
Chalk Mat
Concrete
   Blocks
   Slabs
Masonite
Paper (See Pg. 10)
Sandpaper

Chalk With Liquids

Buttermilk
Canned Milk (with a little liquid starch)
Liquid Starch
Sugar Water (1/3 sugar to 2/3 water)
Water

Accessories

All Size Chalkboards
Holder
Musical Staff Liner

Clean-Up

Cloths
Erasers
Sponges
Water

At The Easel/Chalkboard

EASEL MIX AND MATCH: Offer various chalks with all types of paper.

- White chalk on dark butcher paper cut to the size of your easel.

- Charcoal on easel paper.
  Encourage The Children: "Have you or your parents ever used charcoal for something else?" "What?"

- Colored chalk on classified pages of the newspaper.
  Encourage The Children: "Vanessa, look at your hands. Can you tell what colors of chalk you've been using?" "Latisha, do the colors on your hands match the colors on the paper?"

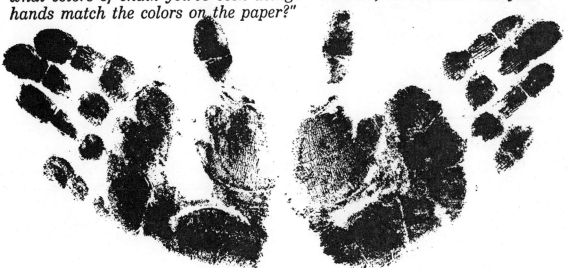

WET AND CHALK: Set water and heavy-duty paper on a table near the easel. Put chalk in the easel tray.

- Put a little water in a bucket along with wide paint brushes. Let a child brush the backside of a piece of wallpaper with water, hang it on the easel, and chalk.

- Put a spray bottle of water and a brownie pan near the easel. Have a child lay a bag in the brownie pan, spray the bag with water, hang it on the easel, and chalk.

- Fill a plastic tub about a quarter of the way with water. Have a child slide his entire piece of construction paper into the water, take it out, gently shake off keep excess water, hang the wet paper on the easel, and chalk.

CHALK AND ERASE: At the large or individual chalk boards, offer the children a variety of chalks with different accessories.

- Put out a different type of chalk with erasers every couple of days.
  Encourage The Children: After they have had opportunities to use several types of chalk, talk about the differences and similarities, what they like and don't like about the different types, and which ones they like to use best and least. "Why?"

- Put a different color piece of chalk in each compartment of a musical staff liner.
  Encourage The Children: As the children are making lines, talk about the colors.

- Have several pieces of Masonite for individual chalk boards along with damp sponges for erasing and small cloths for drying.

EXPERIMENTING WITH CHALK: On successive days hang the same type of paper on the easel, but have a different type of chalk. For example, use large sheets of manilla paper with colored, white, poster, charcoal, and pastel chalks.
Encourage The Children: Compare the different chalks. "Juanita, which colors do they like? Which ones are easiest to hold? Does the poster chalk make wider lines than the other chalks?"

CHALK MARKS: Hang large pieces of paper on the easel. Using all types of chalk, have the children see how many different marks they can make. Show them how to use the tops and sides of their chalk.
Encourage The Children: "Tia, look how dark the color is when you press hard with your chalk." "Paul, you're making lines with the tip of your chalk." "Carol, you're using the side of your chalk." "You're drawing swirls with your chalks."

On The Table/Floor

CHALK MIX AND MATCH: Offer the chalks with papers and other surfaces in a variety of ways.

- Colored chalk on trays. Wipe off with erasers.

- White chalk on bricks or cement blocks. Near the end of each day, let the children wash the bricks with water and a toothbrush, so that the bricks are clean and ready to use again.
EXTENSION: White chalk on sandpaper.
Encourage The Children: Compare chalking on bricks and sandpaper.

- Dark colored chalk on light paper and light colored chalk on dark paper.

DIP AND CHALK: Pour liquid starch into several small containers. Put them around the table. Have a basket of colored chalk and construction paper available. Tell the children to dip their chalk into the starch and then draw with it. Re-dip as the chalk dries. Use a different liquid on another day.
Encourage The Children: Tell the children what liquid is in the containers. Do their chalk drawings look different from the ones they did using dry chalk? "How does the wet chalk feel?"

CHALK AND SMEAR: Tape a large piece of butcher paper to the table or floor. Using any of the chalks, have the children draw whatever they'd like. When finished, they should gently use their fingers and hands to smear their chalk lines and chalk dust around the paper.

59

Outside

CHALK AND CLEAN: Use different chalks on the sidewalk and playground. Clean up in various ways:

- Spray the drawings with a hose.

- Use water and scrub brushes.

- Shuffle the tracings with your gym shoes.

- Let it rain!
  Encourage The Children: *"How does it feel to chalk outside?" "Do you ever chalk outside at your home?" "How do you clean up your chalk drawings at home?"*

MY OWN SPACE: In a quiet, more secluded area of the playground, mark off a space for each child who would like to chalk by himself. Have a variety of chalks available from which he can choose. After he is finished chalking, write his name in his space.

CHALK TRACINGS: Over several weeks, have the children each lie down in an open, but quiet area of the playground. Using poster chalk, make a tracing of each child. Let him add features and color with colored chalk. He can then choose to clean it up or save it for several days.
Encourage The Children: *Watch the tracings each day. What is happening to those which were drawn first?*

... notes for myself ~

ADDITIONAL RESOURCES

- **Everyday Bulletin Boards,** *Wilmes/Moehling.* Borders, murals, backgrounds and other open-ended art for bulletin boards.
- **Exploring Art,** *Wilmes/Wilmes.* 250 open-ended art activities with a display suggestion.
- **Gifts, Cards, Wraps,** *Wilmes/Zavodsky.* Easy presents for children to make and wrap.
- **Mudworks,** *Kohl.* Doughs, modeling mixtures, and more.
- **1,2,3 Art,** *Warren.* 200 open-ended art activities.
- **Scribble Cookies,** *Kohl.* Open-ended art, some new - some familiar.

Blocks

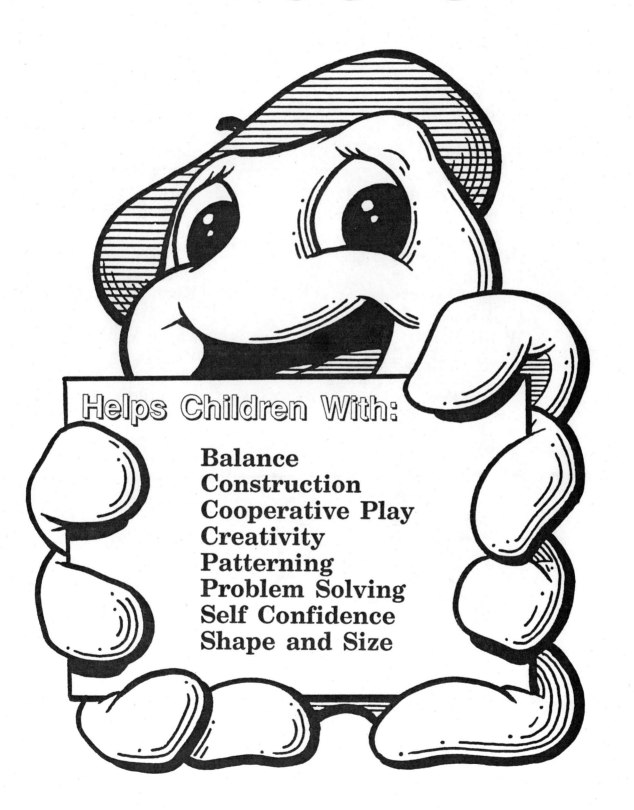

Helps Children With:

Balance
Construction
Cooperative Play
Creativity
Patterning
Problem Solving
Self Confidence
Shape and Size

Blocks
Supply List

Blocks

Cardboard Blocks
Foam Blocks
Giant Snap and Lock Blocks
Giant Tinker Toys
Hollow Wooden Blocks
Lincoln Logs
Super Blocks
Unit Blocks
Waffle Blocks

Accessories

Barn
Boats
Cars
Carpet Tubes
Community Helpers
Construction Hats
Dolls
Farm Animals
Fence
Large Vehicles
People
Posters of Simple Buildings
Puppets
Ramps
Riding Vehicles
Safety Vehicles
Sets of Small Blocks
Stuffed Animals
Traffic Signs
Trains
Trucks
Visors
Wagon
Wheel Barrow
Zoo Animals

Clean-Up

Shelving Units with Labeled Shelves

HANDY HINT:

MAKE YOUR BLOCKS: Collect sturdy shoe boxes. Tape the lids on. Add them to your block shelf.

Building Without Accessories

BLOCKS MIX AND MATCH: Offer a variety of large blocks with which the children can safely build as they choose.

- **Labeling** - Label each block shelf with the actual-size pattern of the block which belongs on it.
  Encourage The Children: "Rose, let me help you put your blocks away. I'll hand them to you, and you put them on the shelves." Watch as children put their blocks away. Remind them to neatly pile the blocks on the different shelves. "Thank you, Jeff, for stacking the blocks so carefully."

- **Watch and Comment** - Stand in or close to the area where a child or group of children is building. As they are building, make short, quiet comments or ask questions.
  Encourage The Children: "Greg, tell me about your building." "You are really building a giant structure with those cardboard blocks! Are you planning to use all of them? Let me know when you have finished." "John, you're having so much fun with the blocks. Can I just stand here and watch you for awhile?"

- **Build With Children** - You can build your own structure or work with a child.

  Encourage The Children: As you are building, gently introduce new structures, such as towers, roads, bridges, fences, walls, and so on. Ask a child, "Can we use this type of block?" "Do we need long or short blocks?"

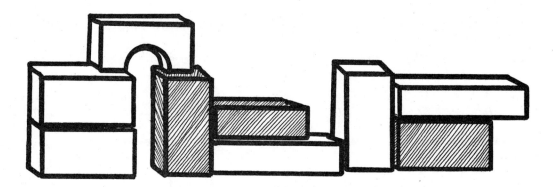

- **Build and Label** - After the children have worked on their structures, ask them if they have a name for what they built and if they would like you to write the name on a giant card. Get a piece of posterboard, write the name down, and set the card on the structure.

My House

- **Do Not Disturb** - If children are still working on a building structure when it is time to stop for the day, ask them whether they want to clean it up or continue to work on it tomorrow. If they want to continue it tomorrow, put a "Do Not Disturb" sign near their blocks.
Encourage The Children: As you're setting the sign by their structure, ask them what they think they are going to add to it. Tell other children about the structure/s being left in the area.

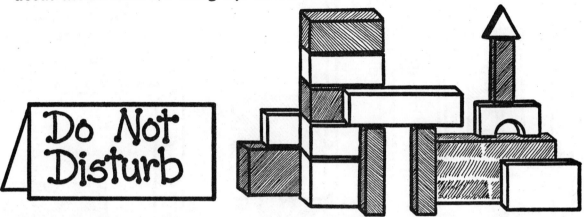

- **Simple Posters** - Hang a simple, large poster of a building. Change it every 3, 4, or 5 weeks.
VARIATION: While on a walk around your neighborhood, take photographs of the different buildings. Mount each picture on a piece of construction paper and hang several at a time on a wall in the block area.
Encourage The Children: "Alma, look at the building. Does it look tall to you?" "What do you think people do in that building?" "Do you see all of the bricks in that building? We have blocks that look like bricks." "Kevin, what do you think this is a photograph of? How can you tell?"

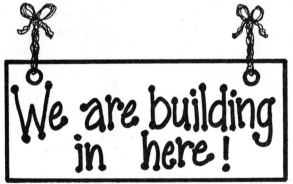

- **Building In Progress** - Hang a large sign from the ceiling at the entrance to the block area.
Encourage The Children: "The sign says that there is building going on in here. Greg, tell me what you're building." "Jasmine, you are using so many different blocks. Tell me about all of them."

- **Smile, You're Building** - Take children's photographs as they are building. Mount them on posterboard. Hang the display in the block area. Let children take their photos home when they want. Continue adding more as time goes on.
Encourage The Children: "What were you building, Bobby, when I took this picture?" "Emily, you were building a long line of blocks. Look!"

•Build and Show-Off - While a child is working on a block project, ask him if he would like you to make a name card which he can place by the building after it is finished. If he says, "Yes," make a name card. As each child finishes, he can put his card someplace on or near the structure.

•Build and Dictate - After the children have finished a simple or elaborate building structure, ask them if they would like to tell you a story about it. Have a large piece of chart paper and a marker handy. As the children tell you about their structure, write down what they say. Hang the story on a wall in the block area.

●**Building Buddies** - Make construction worker headbands which the children can wear while they are building. Duplicate the insignias and staple them on 2" posterboard bands.

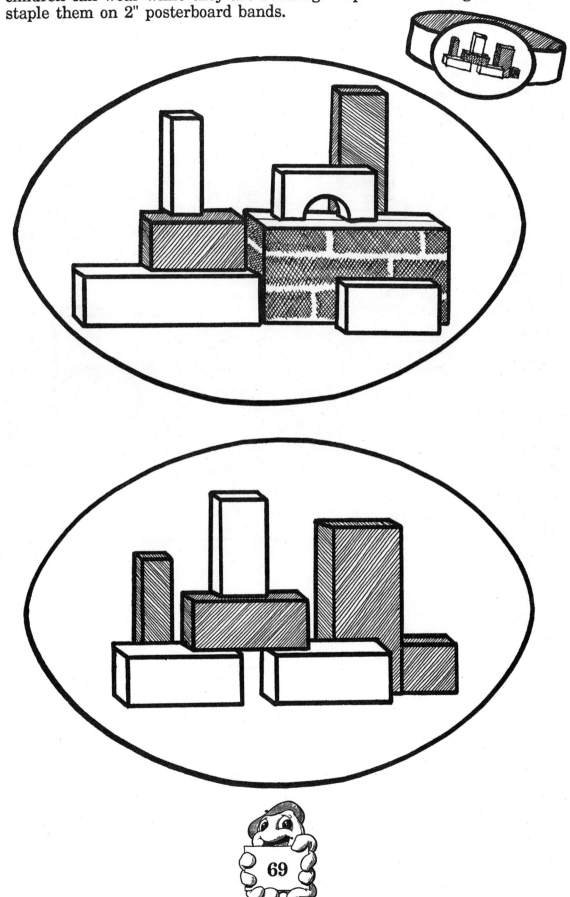

BLOCK TOWERS: Encourage the children to build tower-type structures.

● Have the children build towers which reach from the floor to different parts of their bodies, such as a tower to their knees, or to their waists.

After a child has built a tower, count the number of blocks that he has used.
Encourage The Children*: Touch each block as you count together. "You have 8 blocks in your tower, Michael." After counting the blocks in a child's tower, ask him how many there were. "How many blocks did we count in your tower, Dick?"*

● Using different size blocks, build towers which stand next to each other.
Encourage The Children *- "Are our towers the same height, Joshua?" "What tower was built with the tallest blocks?" "Shortest blocks?" "Let's build another tower. You choose the type of block to use."*

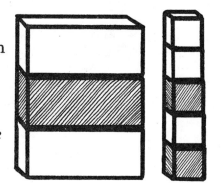

● Alternating blocks, build a tower with a child. Let him start by putting the first block on the floor, you put the next one on top, and so on. Decide together how tall your tower should be.
Encourage The Children *- "Our tower is getting tall, Emily. Let's count the blocks we've used." "James, should we stop building or should we add several more blocks to our tower?"*

● Using small blocks, have children build towers on the palm of their hands. Maybe they would like to work together with one child holding out his palm and the other one building on it.

BLOCK MEASURING: Use blocks to measure different things in the room.

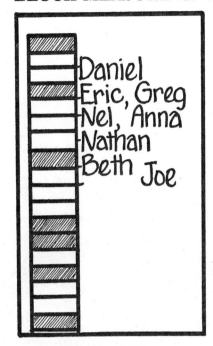

• Measure all of the children to see how many blocks high each one is. Make a simple chart of their 'block heights' and post it in the area.

To make the chart get a long piece of butcher paper. Using a marker, draw a block tower taller than your tallest child. Hang it on a wall flush to the floor.

During the next several weeks, have each child stand by the tower. Put your finger on the block which shows his height. Have him stand away from the chart. Count the blocks together, then write his name on the chart.

Encourage The Children - *After several children have been measured, talk about the chart. "Who is the tallest?" "Shortest?" "Who are the same heights?" Count the blocks for different children. "Let's see, Betty is 1, 2, 3 and part of the fourth block tall."*

• Using one type and size block, measure different things in the room. One way to do this is to put lots of one type and size block in a wagon or large box. When a child wants to measure something, he pulls the wagon over to the piece, lays blocks end-to-end along the object to be measured, and then counts the blocks. You could make a chart to record all of the measurements.

• Using one type and size block, measure different distances in your room. For example, measure how many blocks it is from the door to the cubbies, or from the climber to the easel, or from the waste basket to the bulletin board.

71

BLOCK DIRECTIONS: Sit with one or more children in the block area. Give them different directions using the blocks.

"Sam, count out 5 blocks and use them to build a tower."

"Carol, build a zig-zag road."

"Yolanda, pick out 3 blocks and build a bridge."

"Kevin, use a different type of block than Sam did and build a very short tower next to his."

"Carin and Catherine, you work together and build a fence around Sam's and Kevin's towers."

BLOCK TWINS: Sit with one or more children in the block area. You build some type of structure and let others copy it.

- You build a simple structure using the same blocks. Have a child duplicate it right alongside yours.

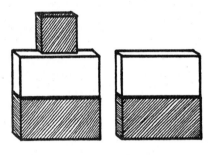

- You construct a simple structure and have a child build his twin structure away from yours.

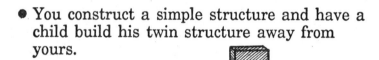

- Let a child build the first structure. You/other children make twins of it. ***Encourage The Children*** - *"Jamie, you build the first structure. Here are 4 blocks to use."* Another time talk to yourself as you're trying to copy a structure. *"Judy used 3 long blocks on the bottom of her building. Let's start there. Then she stacked 2 cylinders in the middle. 1, 2. Last she carefully laid a block on top of the cylinders to make a bridge. Good, we did it! Let's look at Judy's again and see if ours matches hers perfectly."*

- Build more complex structures to copy.

BLOCKS BOX: Have a large box. Cover it with decorated paper and label it 'Blocks Box.' Every couple of weeks fill it with a different assortment of blocks. Put it on the block shelf. Plan special activities to do with these blocks.

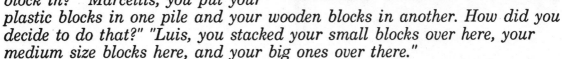

● Put a variety of different blocks in the 'Blocks Box.' Have the children lay out all of the blocks and then sort them into groups they've chosen.

Encourage The Children - "Sally, you have 3 piles of blocks. How did you know which pile to put each block in?" "Marcellis, you put your plastic blocks in one pile and your wooden blocks in another. How did you decide to do that?" "Luis, you stacked your small blocks over here, your medium size blocks here, and your big ones over there."

● Put the same type but different sizes of a block into the 'Blocks Box.' Have the children stack the blocks in a series from large to small or small to large.

END-TO-END: Have children build 'end-to-end' structures.

● Put several long pieces of colored tape on the floor in the block area. Have a child lay blocks along the tape.
Encourage The Children - "Terrell, let's put blocks along this red tape. You pick the type of block." "Stephen, you are really working hard. You are making your third layer of blocks on the green tape."

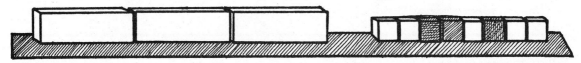

● Have a ball of heavy, colored yarn and a pair of scissors. After a child has built an end-to-end structure, measure it with yarn. To do this, have the child hold the yarn at one end of the structure, while you roll it out to the other end and cut it. Let the child decide if he wants to take the yarn home or hang it in the block area. If he is taking his yarn home, roll it up and put it in a sandwich bag. If he is keeping it at school, tack it to a chart.

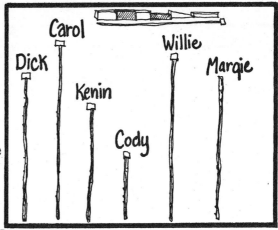

BLOCK BALANCE: Give a child two blocks of the same type but different sizes blocks and have him balance them one on top of the other. Can he balance the two together another way? Try more blocks after awhile.

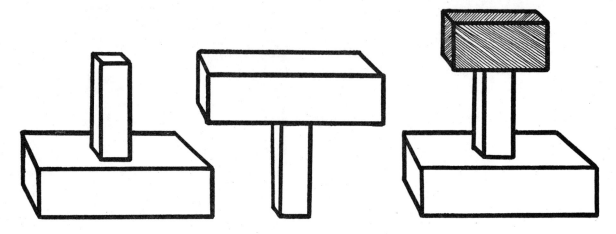

SHAPES WITHIN BLOCKS: As a child is using blocks, have him hold one in his hand. Have him look at one side of the 3-D block. Using your index finger draw a line around the shape. Let him trace the shape. Turn the block to another side. Repeat. Do the activity again with different blocks.

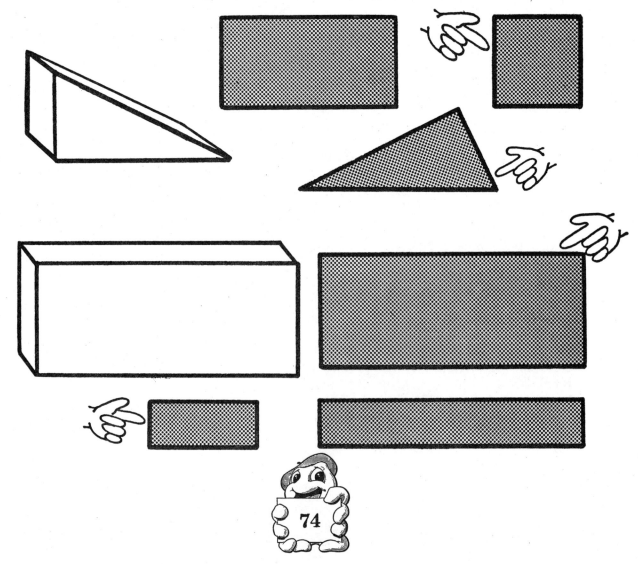

74

Building With Accessories

BLOCKS/ACCESSORIES MIX AND MATCH: Offer a variety of accessories for the children to use with the blocks. Rotate the accessories to stimulate continuous play and interest. Have only a few out at a time, so that the children will not be overwhelmed.

● Safety vests for children to wear, plus traffic signs, cars, and trucks.

MAKE SIMPLE PAPER BAG SAFETY VESTS

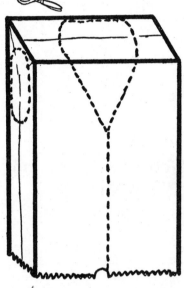
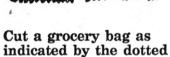

Cut a grocery bag as indicated by the dotted lines.

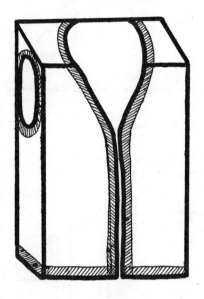

Tape all of the edges of the bag with heavy-duty tape.

Glue the 'Safety Patrol' patch to the back side of the vest.

- Barn, farm animals, people.

  Encourage The Children - *Suggest that the children use blocks to build fences and fields for the animals. "You've got a long fence, Jeremy. What animals are in your field?"*

MAKE A SIMPLE CARDBOARD BOX BARN

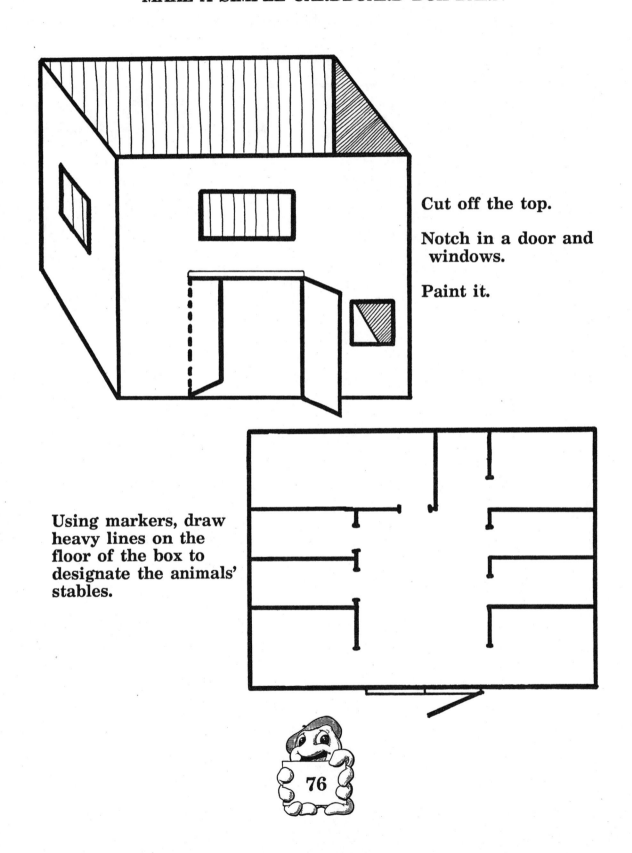

Cut off the top.

Notch in a door and windows.

Paint it.

Using markers, draw heavy lines on the floor of the box to designate the animals' stables.

- Construction hats or headbands, large trucks, and wheel barrows.
  Encourage The Children - *"Where are you going with that load of bricks, Willie?" "I like the way you are driving your load so safely." "What are you going to build with all of those blocks, Tira?"*

Duplicate the insignias and staple them to posterboard bands.

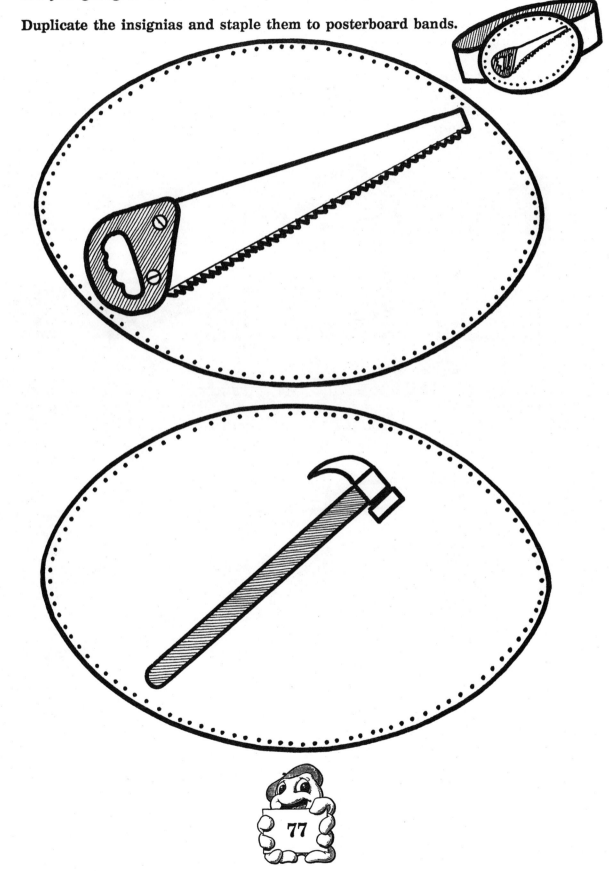

● Boards, small cars, and people.

- Have the children build ramps at different angles and drive cars up and down them.

- Place cars at the tops of several ramps and let them go. Where did the cars stop? Did any car fall off its ramp? Why?

- Build a highway system with the children.

- Put people in the cars and take a trip. Where are they going? What are they going to do?

● Dolls and stuffed friends.
Encourage The Children - *"Alice, you're building a home for your dolls. Show me where they're going to sleep." "That's a big area, Luis. Whose going to live in there?" "You need a small blanket, Greg? Get one from the housekeeping area."*

● Zoo animals, people, buses, trucks, and cars. In a secluded space of the block area, make a small parking lot with colored tape which could be part of a zoo.
Encourage The Children: "Are you building areas for the animals? Which animals will live in your zoo?" "What animals do you see when you go to the zoo? Which one is your favorite?" "Do you eat picnic lunches at the zoo? What do you have?"

● Community helpers, a telephone, fire truck, ambulance, police car, and a piece of rubber hose.
Encourage The Children: "Betty, tell me what you're building. Be careful, I don't want you to get hurt." "Sami, why are you getting the fire hose? Let me help you put out the fire in your house." "Let's build a hospital. One of our dolls is sick and another one has a broken arm. Have any of you ever been in the hospital?"

ON THE ROAD AGAIN: Use colored tape and make simple roads on the floor. Add safety signs and a wide variety of vehicles.
Encourage The Children: *"I see you built a building at the end of the road, Joey. What is it?" "Samantha you built a giant parking lot. I bet you can park all of the cars, trucks, and buses in it."*

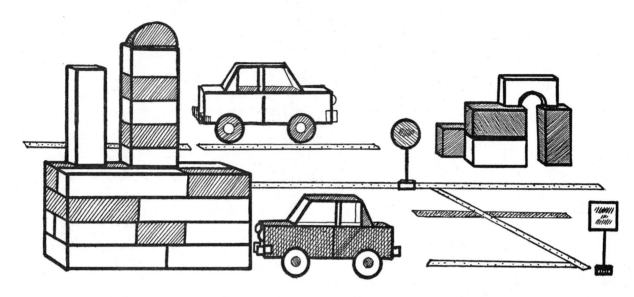

FIELD TRIP FOLLOW-UP: At the children's eye level, hang a poster representing the place you went, such as one of a giraffe from the zoo or vegetables from the grocery store. You could add several buses, zoo animals, foods, or other accessories depending on the trip.

Zoo Trip

BLOCK PATTERNS: Draw actual size block patterns on large pieces of paper. Have the children match the shapes with real blocks.

- Draw patterns of individual blocks on large pieces of tagboard. Lay the tagboard on the floor and let the children place real blocks on the drawn ones.
Encourage The Children - *"Kevin, find the block which matches the shape I'm pointing to. Now find this one." "You've matched all of the blocks, Juan. Good for you!" "Lauri, you matched all of the block shapes yesterday. Would you like to do it again today?"*

- Draw different series of block patterns on pieces of posterboard. Start with an easy series and get more difficult. Hang one series at a time low on the wall. Have the children look at the series and then copy it on the floor with real blocks.

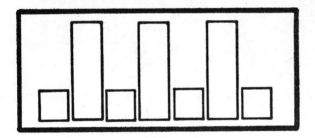 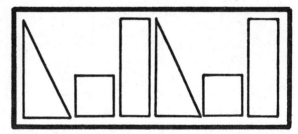

- Using blocks, draw actual structures on pieces of posterboard. Lay one or two on the floor and let children match real blocks to the pattern/s.

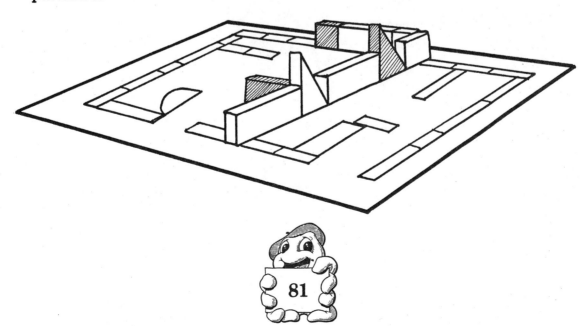

Outside

NEW CONSTRUCTION SITE: Put a set of blocks in several wagons. Pull them outside. Enjoy building in a shady area.

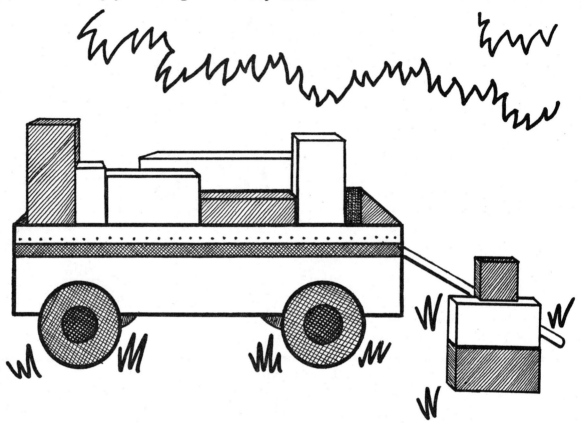

TENT FUN: Construct a quick tent by draping a sheet over an outside table. Lay a blanket inside of the tent to sit on. Put a set of small blocks in the tent. Encourage children to sit inside and build.

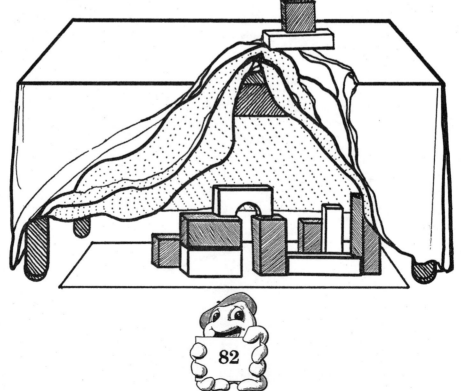

... notes for myself ~

ADDITIONAL RESOURCES

- **The Block Book,** *NAEYC.* History, philosophy, and activities for block play.
- **Creative Curriculum,** *Dodge.* Seven learning centers, including blocks.

Dramatic Play

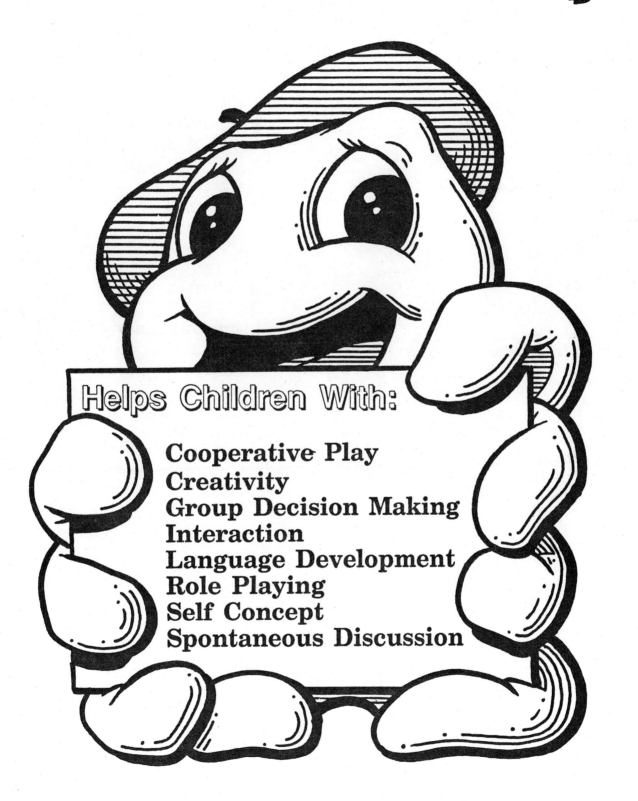

Helps Children With:

Cooperative Play
Creativity
Group Decision Making
Interaction
Language Development
Role Playing
Self Concept
Spontaneous Discussion

Dramatic Play
Supply List

Equipment

Balance Beam
Bench
Chairs
Cots
Full Length Mirror
Hoops
Record Player
Riding Toys
Scooter
Table
Tumbling Mat
Wagons
Waste Basket

Clean-Up

Broom
Dustpan
Sponges
Towels

Clothes

Aprons
Beach Jacket
Clown Suits
Hair Nets
Hats
Headbands
Leotards
Purses
Shorts
Sunglasses
Sun Visors
Swimming Suits
T-Shirts
Visor
White Shirts
Work Shirts
Wrist Bands

86

Accessories

HANDY HINT:

PROP BOX: Put the props and accessories for each set-up in a special box. Easy to store.

Backpack
Baton
Beach Towels
Biscuit Cutters
Boots
Camera
Cars
Cash Registers
Clothesline
Cookie sheets
Cymbals
Dowel Rods
Elastic
Flashlight
Funnel
Guitar
Hose
Ice Cream Buckets
Ice Cream Scoops
Life Preservers
Loaf Pans
Magazines
Maracas
Menus
Microphones
Muffin Cups
Muffin Tins
Music Books
Paper Tablets
Paper Towels
Picnic Baskets
Pitcher
Pizza Boards
Pom-Poms
Popcorn Boxes
Pots & Pans
Punching Bag
Raincoats
Rags
Rolling Pins

Ruler
Safety Cones
Shoe Boxes
Shoe Horns
Shoes
Sleeping Bags
Sponges
Spray Bottles
Squeegee
Steering Wheel
Stethoscope
Straws
Streamers
Stuffed Animals
Suntan Lotion
Syringe
Tambourine
Tongue Depressors
Trays
Trucks
Vehicles
Wash Cloth
Xylophone

BEACH

TAKE A FIELD TRIP: Before setting up the beach in your classroom, have a picnic at your local beach or park with a swimming pool.

CLASSROOM VISITOR: While the children are enjoying the beach, ask a life guard to visit the children. Have him/her bring the rescue equipment and tell the children how she/he uses it. If there is a film on water safety, show it.

Fill a bucket with plaster of paris. Stick a dowel rod and plastic flowers into it and let dry. Tape your flag to the rod. Set it at the entrance to the beach.

BEACH SCENE
- Hang a huge sun and clouds from the ceiling.
- Have a large tub of water to sail boats in.
- Mark off a swimming area with blue tape.
- Set a life guard chair by the area with pails and shovels.

BEACH PROPS
- Beach chairs
- Life preservers for swimming.
- Picnic basket, blanket, plates, etc.
- Safety cones for high tide
- Suntan lotion
- Towels to lie on

BEACH CLOTHES
- Beach jackets
- Boys, girls swimming suits which they can pull on over their clothes
- Sun glasses
- Sun visors
- Sweat bands

Encourage The Children:

Talk about the times children have gone to the beach.

Ask the children if they swim in pools near their homes. What do they do in the water?

BUS RIDE

TAKE A FIELD TRIP: Before setting up the bus ride in your classroom, get a bus schedule and take your children for a ride to a nearby park. Have a picnic, play for awhile, and take a bus ride back to your school.

CLASSROOM VISITOR: During the time that your bus ride is set up, ask a bus driver to come to your classroom. Ask him/her to wear his/her uniform. While there, s/he can talk about where s/he drives the bus, who rides on it, and what s/he likes best about his/her job.

BUS RIDE SCENE
- Chairs for bus seats
- Special chair for driver

BUS RIDE PROPS
- Steering wheel
- Stuffed animals
- Tickets for passengers to wear around their necks while riding

BUS RIDE CLOTHES
- Hat or headband for the driver
- Shirt for the driver
- Purses for the passengers

See page 88 for directions to make the container. Tape the 'Bus Stop' sign to the dowel rod. Set it near the bus.

Encourage The Children:

"Rolando, give the bus driver your money. She will give you a ticket to wear. When you get off, give it back to her."

"Bus driver Ti, I would like to get off at the Elgin stop please. I'm going to go shopping at the mall."

"Bryant, where are you going today?"

CAMPGROUND

TAKE A FIELD TRIP: Before setting up the campground in your classroom, visit a camping store in your locale. Have the store keeper show the children the tents, the sleeping bags, and the camping equipment.

CLASSROOM VISITOR: During the time that the campground is set up in your classroom, ask one of your parents who likes to camp to visit your children. If s/he has slides or a video of a trip maybe s/he would share it with the children.

TRAVEL SCENE
- Circle of rocks with several logs
- Cots
- Taped off area for a fishing pond
- Tent

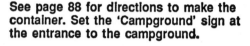

See page 88 for directions to make the container. Set the 'Campground' sign at the entrance to the campground.

TRAVEL PROPS
- Backpack
- Camera
- Clothesline and clothespins
- Flashlight
- Posterboard fish (See Sand/Water for pattern.)
- Pots to cook over fire
- Several fishing poles
- Sleeping bags
- Stuffed animals

TRAVEL CLOTHES
- Raincoats
- Shorts
- Sunglasses
- Sweatband
- Swimming suits

Encourage The Children:

Sit with the children at the camp site and sing familiar songs

Pretend to cook over the fire.

Go fishing. What kind of fish are you catching? Red ones?

CAR WASH

TAKE A FIELD TRIP: Before setting up the car wash in the classroom, walk to your nearest car wash facility. Have the attendant show the children how cars are washed.

CLASSROOM VISITOR: One day while the car wash is set up, ask several parents to volunteer as "car wash attendants." Move the car wash outside and clean all of the big riding toys and vehicles.

CAR WASH SCENE
- Parking lot for vehicles waiting to be washed
- Table with wash tubs - one half full of soapy water, the other with clear water

CAR WASH PROPS
- All sizes of cars, trucks, and other vehicles
- Cash register
- Pieces of hose
- Rags for drying cars
- Sponges
- Spray bottles

CAR WASH CLOTHES
- Hats
- Shirts

See page 88 for directions to make the container. Set the 'Car Wash' sign at the entrance to the area.

Encourage The Children:

"Netti, what kind of truck are you washing? It looks like it hauls big loads."

Remind the children to pay for their car wash.

Talk about times when they have been through a car wash with their moms/dads.

CLOWN SHOW

TAKE A FIELD TRIP: Before setting up this clown show in your classroom, take your class to see a local parade. Check your community calendar - maybe your high school has a homecoming parade, the citizens have a holiday parade, or a special event is going on in your town.

CLASSROOM VISITOR: During the time that your clown show is set up, ask a local clown, actor, or actress to come into your classroom. You might ask the clown to come dressed except for his/her make-up. Let the clown put his/her make-up on for the children.

CLOWN DRESSING ROOM SCENE
- Clown clothes
- Clown hats/headbands
- Full length mirror
- Table and chair for make-up
- Have a mirror for children to see their faces as they apply their make-up.

See page 88 for directions to make the container. Tape the 'Clown Show' sign to the dowel rod. Set it near the entrance.

CLOWN SHOW SCENE
- Balance beam or tumbling mat to show off clown tricks
- Chairs to view the show
- Hoops

CLOWN PROPS
- Baton
- Circus music
- Streamers

CLOWN MAKE-UP
You'll Need:

4T Shortening	¼t Glycerin
10T Cornstarch	Food Coloring
2T Flour	

To Make: Using a rubber spatula, blend the first three ingredients on a smooth, flat surface to form a paste. Add glycerin and blend again. Divide the paste into smaller portions. Mix each portion with a few drops of food coloring for a variety of colors. Use your fingers to apply the make-up on each child's face. Remove the 'greasepaint' with cold cream, shortening, or baby oil.

DOCTOR'S OFFICE

TAKE A FIELD TRIP: Before setting up a doctor's office, take a trip to the emergency room of your hospital.

CLASSROOM VISITOR: During the time that the doctor's office is set up, ask a doctor, nurse, or paramedic to come to your classroom. Have the person bring his/her medical bag and show the children how the basic equipment and supplies are used. If there is time, let each child listen to his heart with a stethoscope.

DOCTOR'S WAITING ROOM SCENE
- Appointment book, pencil
- Chairs for patients
- Desk and chair
- Magazines to read
- Plants

Hang a large posterboard sign at the entrance to the doctor's office.

DOCTOR'S OFFICE SCENE
- Medical tray with supplies
- Table covered with a sheet for examining
- Waste basket (throw away tongue depressors, straws, etc.)

DOCTOR'S PROPS
- Large pieces of white fabric cut into triangles for slings.
- Plastic thermometer or coffee stir sticks/straws
- Stethoscope
- Strips of cotton for large bandaging
- Syringe for shots
- Tongue depressors
- Wash cloth

Fold the long edge of 9"x12" piece of paper up 2" Fold the top corners into a cone shape. Staple closed.

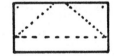 

DOCTOR'S CLOTHES
- Hats - ask your local hospital to donate disposable hats/gowns
- Nurse hats
- White shirts

Encourage The Children:

Let boys and girls be doctors, nurses, receptionists, patients, and parents bringing in children.

DONUT SHOP

TAKE A FIELD TRIP: Before setting up the donut shop in the classroom, walk over to a local bakery or donut shop. Watch a baker, cake decorator, or donut maker.

CLASSROOM VISITOR: During the time that the donut shop is set up, ask a baker to come into your classroom and show the children the different tools she/he uses to make donuts, cakes, muffins, etc.

DONUT SHOP SCENE
- Table for display and paying
- Table for making bakery goods
- Table and chairs to eat donuts

See page 88 for directions to make the container. Set the 'Donut Shop' sign at the entrance to the shop.

DONUT SHOP PROPS
- Biscuit cutters
- Cash register
- Cookie sheets
- Cups for drinking
- Hang giant donuts and muffins from ceiling.
- Loaf pans
- Muffin cups
- Muffin tins
- Plates for donuts
- Playdough (See recipe in the Art Center.)
- Rolling pins
- Trays for displaying the bakery goods

DONUT SHOP CLOTHES
- Baker's hat or headband
- Hair nets
- Visor
- White shirts

Encourage The Children:

Talk about what kinds of donuts everyone likes.

Be a baker and help the children make and decorate cakes.

Sit with the children and have a donut.

GAS STATION

TAKE A FIELD TRIP: Before setting up the gas station in the classroom, walk over to a local gas station. Have an attendant show the children around the station. See the gas pumps, air pump, and displays of oil and other car products.

CLASSROOM VISITOR: During the time that the gas station is open in your classroom, ask an attendant or car mechanic to visit your classroom and tell your children about car care.

GAS STATION SCENE
- Scooter
- Several tall narrow boxes for pumps (Add a rubber hose for the nozzle.)
- Small riding toys
- Table for paying
- Wagon

GAS STATION PROPS
- Cash register
- Dish of shallow water
- Funnel
- Paper towels
- Rags
- Sponges
- Squeegee
- Stuffed animals for passengers

GAS STATION CLOTHES
- Baseball type hats or headbands
- Work shirts

See page 88 for directions to make the container. Set the 'Gas Station' sign at the entrance to the station.

Encourage The Children:

Drive your vehicle into the gas station. Let the attendant fill your tank and wash your windows.

Have the children check the oil in each car.

Someone may need his car washed also. Be ready.

ICE CREAM PARLOR

TAKE A FIELD TRIP: Before setting up the ice cream parlor in your classroom, walk to the closest ice cream shop and let the children order cones. Sit at the shop and enjoy the delicious flavors together. After that, have one of the workers show you around.

CLASSROOM VISITOR: During the time that your ice cream parlor is set up, ask several parents to come in and help you have an ice cream social at school. Buy ice cream and several additions like raisins, pineapples, bananas, and toppings. Get bowls and spoons. Let the adults scoop the ice cream and let children sprinkle on the extras.

ICE CREAM PARLOR SCENE
- Giant posterboard ice cream cones hanging from the ceiling
- Several small tables and chairs
- Table to make ice cream treats
- Waste basket to throw straws away

ICE CREAM PARLOR PROPS
- Cash register
- Colored pom-poms for ice cream scoops
- Menus
- Paper cones
- Ice cream dishes
- Ice cream scoop
- Napkins
- Spoons
- Straws
- Trays to serve ice cream on
- 5 gallon ice cream pails

ICE CREAM PARLOR CLOTHES
- Aprons
- Hats or visors
- White shirts

Encourage The Children:

Talk about favorite flavors.

Tape the 'Ice Cream Parlor' sign to the back of a cabinet near the entrance.

Glue brown or beige cones to different colored scoops. Have the scoops back-to-back on each cone.

IN THE GYM

TAKE A FIELD TRIP: Before setting up the gym in your classroom, take the children to a local Nautilus, gym, YMCA/YWCA, or park district weight and exercise facility.

CLASSROOM VISITOR: During the time that your gym is set up, ask a local aerobics or gym teacher to come into your classroom. Ask the teacher to talk about the importance of exercising and eating nutritious foods. The teacher might also have time to exercise with the children.

GYM LOCKER SCENE
- Bench
- Full length mirror
- Table for gym clothes

GYM SCENE
- Balance beam
- Exercise and warm-up charts (Found in the Large Motor section)
- Exercise records
- Record player
- Tumbling mat
- Wide pieces of elastic cord taped securely to the back of a cabinet for children to pull - relax with

Our Gym

Hang a large posterboard sign at the entrance to the gym.

GYM PROPS
- Disposable cups for drinking water
- Pitcher of drinking water
- Punching bag
- Small towels
- Two dowel rods for free weights
- Wrist weights

GYM CLOTHES
- Belts
- Headbands
- Leotards or one piece bathing suits
- Shorts, which children can wear over their clothes
- T-Shirts
- Wristbands

Encourage The Children:

Exercise with the children.

Talk with the children about taking care of their bodies by eating good food and exercising.

MOVIE THEATER

TAKE A FIELD TRIP: Before setting up the movie theatre in your classroom, take the children to see a matinee at your local theatre. While there, have popcorn.

CLASSROOM VISITOR: During the time that the movie theater is set up, ask your librarian to come and visit your class. Ask him/her to bring a book/filmstrip to read and/or show the children. Have popcorn and juice.

MOVIE SCENE
- Chairs for the theater
- Table for refreshments
- Table to sell tickets
- Television set
- Video recorder

MOVIE PROPS
- Cash registers (2)
- Cups for drinks
- Flashlight for usher
- Popcorn boxes
- Short children's story videos
- Tickets for patrons to wear while watching the movie

MOVIE CLOTHES
- Aprons for snack attendants
- Hat for snack attendants
- Jacket for usher
- Shirt for ticket taker

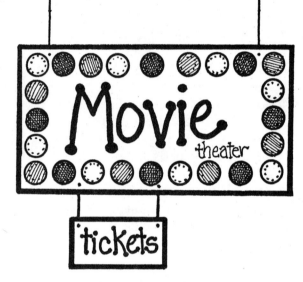

Cut colored circle for lights; glue them to the sign, and hang it from the ceiling over the ticket table.

Encourage The Children:

Partially through the movie have an intermission. Serve popcorn and juice from refreshment stand. Talk with the children about who is in the movie and what is happening.

"Lamar, who do you like best in the movie? Why?"

Talk about movies children see at home. Do they go to the video store with their moms/dads?

MUSIC STUDIO

TAKE A FIELD TRIP: Before setting up the music studio in the classroom, visit a local music store or studio where children take music lessons. Arrange for the children to hear different types of music and see instruments being used.

CLASSROOM VISITOR: During the time that your studio is operating, invite one of your local high schools small bands to visit your children. Let the high school students show the children their instruments. Maybe each visiting student could also play his/her instrument.

MUSIC STUDIO SCENE
- Music Easels
- Record player
- Table for instruments

MUSIC STUDIO PROPS
- Cymbals
- Guitar
- Maracas
- Microphones
- Music books
- Speakers
- Tambourine
- Xylophone

MUSIC STUDIO CLOTHES
- Hats
- Headbands
- Shirts

Encourage The Children:

"Juan, where did you learn to dance?"

"Marce, does your older sister play the guitar?"

"I hear the band. I'm going to dance."

Tape the 'Music Studio' banner to the back of a cabinet near the entrance.

Make microphones by pushing styrofoam snowballs onto wooden dowel rods.

PICNIC

TAKE A FIELD TRIP: Before setting up the picnic grounds in your classroom, pack a picnic snack or lunch for the children along with several toys such as beach balls and ropes. Put the food and toys in a wagon and walk to the nearest park. Have a picnic under a big tree or in a designated picnic area.

CLASSROOM VISITOR: During the time that your picnic is set up, invite a forest ranger to talk with the children. Have him/her talk to the children about fires, picnic safety, and activities in the park.

PICNIC SCENE
- Blanket
- Chairs
- Lawn chairs
- Small grill or stone fireplace
- Table with a picnic table cloth on it.

PICNIC PROPS
- Binoculars
- Food
- Napkins
- Picnic basket
- Plates
- Small balls
- Tongs with long handles for roasting hot dogs over the grill
- Tableware

PICNIC CLOTHES
- Backpack
- Baseball caps
- Shorts
- Sunglasses
- T-shirts
- Visors

See Page 88 for directions to make the container. Tape the 'Picnic' sign to the dowel rod. Set it at the entrance to the picnic grounds.

Encourage The Children:

Talk about what children eat when they go on picnics. How do they carry their food? What do they drink?

Grill hot dogs with the children.

PIZZA PARLOR

TAKE A FIELD TRIP: Before setting up the pizza parlor in your classroom, take the children to a pizza restaurant in your community. If possible, have one of the pizza cooks show the children how to make pizzas. Stay for lunch.

CLASSROOM VISITOR: One day during the time that your pizza parlor is set up, order pizza to be delivered to your classroom. Ask the delivery person to come in and tell the children how s/he carries pizzas in his/her car. How do the pizzas stay hot?

Hang a large posterboard sign at the entrance to the "Pizza Parlor."

PIZZA PARLOR SCENE
- Box for an oven
- Several tables with chairs
- Table to make pizza

PIZZA PARLOR PROPS
- Cash register
- Menus
- Order pads and pencils
- Pizza boards or cut posterboard circles
- Pizza ingredients cut from posterboard
- Rolling pins
- Shakers for parmesan cheese
- Sponges to wipe tables
- Table settings
- Trays to serve pizza on

PIZZA PARLOR CLOTHES
- Aprons for servers
- Hat or hair net for cooks
- White shirts for cooks

Encourage The Children:

Sit with the children and eat a pizza. What ingredients are on it? What are you drinking with your pizza?

Take turns being the pizza chef. Roll out the dough, add the cheese, sauce, and main ingredients.

Ask the waiter or waitress what ingredients come on the pizza.

THE MALL*

TAKE A FIELD TRIP: Before setting up any one of the stores in the mall in your classroom, take a trip to the local mall. Walk around and look at the different stores. Talk about where the children shop and what they buy.

CLASSROOM VISITOR: During the time that the mall is open in your classroom, ask parents to come in and tell the children about what stores they go into and what they buy. If possible ask someone who works at the featured store (such as shoe store) to come and visit.

SHOE STORE SCENE
- Chairs
- Full length mirror
- Posters
- Shelf for storing shoes
- Table for paying

SHOE STORE PROPS
- Boots
- Cash register
- Different shoes, in boxes if possible
- Ruler to measure feet
- Sacks to carry shoes in
- Shoe horns

SHOE STORE CLOTHES
- Backpacks
- Clerk headband
- Purses

See page 88 for directions to make the container. Set the 'Shoe Store' sign at the entrance to the mall.

Encourage The Children:

Let the children try on different kinds of shoes and slippers.

Talk about the shoes that the children's parents wear.

What kinds of shoes do the children wear? When do they wear certain shoes.

* Each time you open the mall, make a new sign and set-up a different store: Grocery, Shoe, Sports, Toy, Pet, Clothing, Hardware, etc.

... notes for myself ~

ADDITIONAL RESOURCES

- **Hats, Hats, and More Hats,** *Stangl.* 70 easy-to-make hats for dramatic play and more.
- **Instant Curriculum,** *Schiller/Rossano.* 9 curriculum areas, including dramatic play.
- **Resources For Dramatic Play,** *Brokering.* 26 easy set-ups from the Fire Station, Post Office, and Pet Store, to a Tea Party.

103

Housekeeping

Helps Children With:

- Conversation
- Cooperative Play
- Family Roles
- Family Chores, Events
- Group Decision Making
- Problem Solving
- Responsibility
- Self Concept

Housekeeping

Supply List

Equipment

Cabinets
Chairs
Cradle
Doll Carriage
Full Length Mirror
High Chair
Hutch
Iron
Ironing Boards
Refrigerator
Rocking Chair
Sink
Stroller
Tables
Waste Baskets

Clothes

Aprons
Birthday Hats
Bracelets
Fancy Dresses
Gardening Gloves
Hats
High Heel Shoes
Men's Coats
Shirts
Shoes
T-Shirts
Ties
Veils

HANDY HINT:

SIT AND TALK: Take every opportunity to sit and talk with the children as they eat, take care of babies, iron, and so on.

Clean-up

Broom
Carpet Sweeper
Dustpan
Mop

Accessories

Artificial Flowers
Baby Bottles
Baby Blankets
Baby Dolls
Baking Sheet
Balloons
Books
Broom
Canes
Cards
Charts
Clothesline
Clothespins
Crutches
Dirt
Dishes
Doll
Dull Knife
Dust Pan
Eyeglasses
Flower Seeds
Food
Food Containers
Hand Mirror

Household Tools (Plastic)
Lunch Boxes
Mop
Muffin Pan
Music Box
Pots, Pans
Puppets
Puzzles
Radio
Rattles
Rolling Pin
Rug
Scarves
Shaving Cream
Shoe Polish
Sponges
Sprinkling Can
Streamers
Stuffed Animals
Telephones
Toaster
Tongue Depressors
Towels
Trays
Tubs

Quick, Easy Additions

ADD CARDS: Periodically put a set of cards on one of the tables in the area. It might be a deck of playing cards, number cards, picture cards, color cards, etc. Let the children use them in a variety of ways. Some might play alone simply matching pairs, while others might play a game such as "Go Fish."

ADD A CLOTHES LINE: String a short clothesline between two chairs. Have clothespins. Cut out simple clothes from a wrinkle-free fabric. Have a tub of shallow water. Let the children wash and wring out the clothes and then hang them on the clothesline to dry. You might need a towel on the floor to absorb a little bit the dripping water.

ADD BOOKS: Set a special book on a small easel next to a rocking chair or overstuffed pillow. Take the opportunity to read to small groups of children. Change the book depending on the children's interests.

ADD EYE GLASSES: Get several pairs of eye glass frames. Set them on the table so that children can easily wear them.

ADD TELEPHONES: Set two telephones near each other. Dial the phone and say aloud, "Hi, is Dick there?" (Name a child who is playing in the area.) Talk with him for awhile. Then say, "Wait Dick, Liz wants to talk to you." (Name a second child.) Have Liz talk to Dick.

ADD CRUTCHES: Contact your local hospital or clinic and arrange to borrow different types of medical supplies on a regular basis. They might be able to loan you braces, crutches, canes, walkers, etc.
Encourage The Children: "Mona, I saw your mom in the store last night. She was using crutches. What happened?" "Bill, I heard your sister had an accident. Is she OK?"

ADD PLAYDOUGH: Make an extra batch of playdough and set it on a plastic/rubber mat along with a rolling pin, cookie cutters, baking sheet, muffin   pan, and dull knife.

You'll Need:

5 cups of flour
1 cup salt
4T alum
2T vegetable oil
3 cups water
Food coloring (optional)

To Make: Boil the water. Add food coloring to the water if you want a colored dough. Mix all of the dry ingredients in a large bowl. Add the boiling water. Stir together. When the mixture is cool enough, put it on the table and knead it until it is thoroughly mixed.

ADD LUNCH BOXES: Put several lunch boxes on the kitchen counter along with models or pictures of lunch-type food. (Using the patterns, cut out food from posterboard.) Let the children decide which foods should go into the lunch boxes, put them in plastic bags, and make each member of the family a lunch.

Encourage The Children: *"Sam, who's lunch are you making?" "Elden, tell me what you're going to fix for lunch. A sandwich. What kind? What else?"*

ADD TELEVISION: Get a medium size box from the grocery store. Paint it with tempera paint. Cut a large opening in it for the screen. Add dials. Set it on a table along with a television guide and a remote control.
EXTENSION: Set several hand puppets next to the television. Cut an opening in the back so that children can use the television as a puppet stage. Let the children create their own T.V. shows.

ADD PUZZLES: Set a puzzle or two on one of the tables in the area. Sit with the children and put the puzzles together.
Encourage The Children: *"Yolanda, do you and your brothers put puzzles together at home? Where do you do them?" "Jonas, your dad was telling me that he loves puzzles. Does he do a lot of them?" "Here, Asche, this might be the piece you're looking for."*

ADD STUFFED PETS: Get a stuffed dog, a basket for his bed, a brush, a leash, and a food and water bowl. Set those in the area. Let the children care for their pet and brush his hair.
EXTENSION: At other times add different stuffed pets and their associated items.

ADD A RADIO: Set a battery powered radio on a table in the area. (Tape the opening to the batteries closed for safety.) Let the children turn it on and off and listen to the different stations.
Encourage the Children: *"Fedrico, do you listen to the radio at home? What do you like best? Do you listen to any Spanish-speaking stations? What do they play?" "Victor, what does your older brother listen to on the radio? He likes music? What does it sound like? Do you like that music too?"*

ADD A SPECIAL DOLL: Get several special dolls who do not live in the housekeeping center. Every once in awhile, let one or more of them visit the children and other dolls who live there.
Encourage The Children: "We have a visitor today. Robert (doll) has come to play with us. Maybe we can take him for a ride in our wagon."

ADD TOOLS: Get a tool box (basket) and 4-5 child-size tools, such as a screw driver, wrench, hammer, pliers, saw, etc. Have the children 'fix' the furniture in the house.

ADD STROLLERS: Have several strollers/small wagons available for the children to use to walk their babies. You might have several baby blankets or sun hats in case it gets windy or the sun is very bright.

ADD GROCERIES: Get empty cartons and boxes, plastic jars, and cans of food, then stuff the bread bags with paper, and finally gather the imitation food that the children use in the center. Set the bags on the kitchen table at the beginning of the day. Help the children sort and put the food away.
Encourage The Children: As you are putting the groceries away, talk about preparing meals. How would the children use the different foods?

ADD CLOTHES: Get a variety of clothes to iron. Hang each one on a hanger and put it by the iron and ironing board. Let the children iron the clothes and hang them back on the hangers.

ADD BABIES: Put several baby dolls in the area along with accessories such as a high chair, bottle, spoons, food, bowls, a rattle, crib, pajamas, blankets, and a special tub and towel to give the babies baths.

ADD SCENERY: Get a large piece of heavy duty cardboard. Fold the sides so that it easily stands on a table or the floor. Cut a big window in the center. Set it in the housekeeping area. Have the children look outside. What do they see?
EXTENSION: Cut out large, simple posterboard cloud, sun, star, moon, bird, butterfly, and airplane shapes. Hang them from the ceiling so that children can see them when they look out of the window.

ADD CHARTS: On walls or cabinets, tack charts which give the children information about fire prevention, good nutrition, safety, and so on.
Encourage The Children: For example, duplicate the food chart, glue it to a piece of colored construction paper, and hang it on the refrigerator door. Talk with the children about the foods they eat each day.

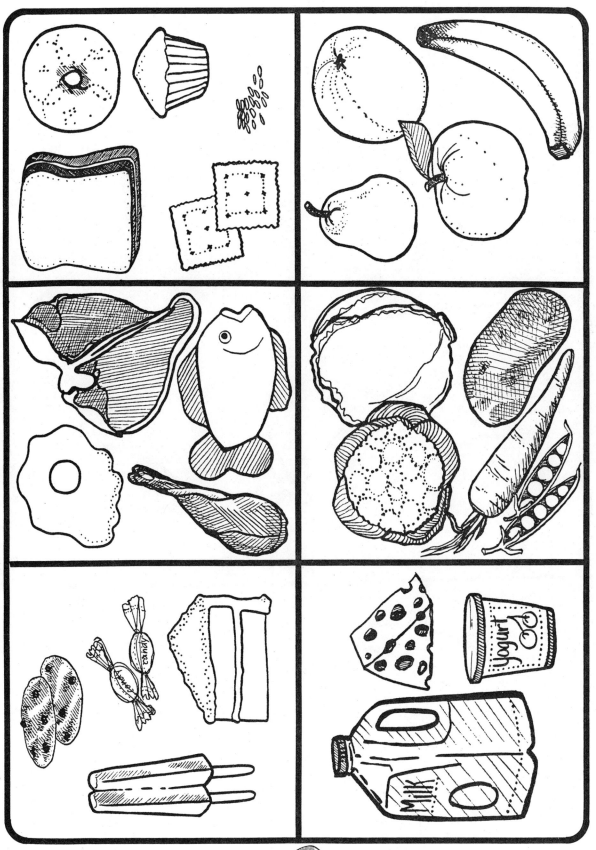

113

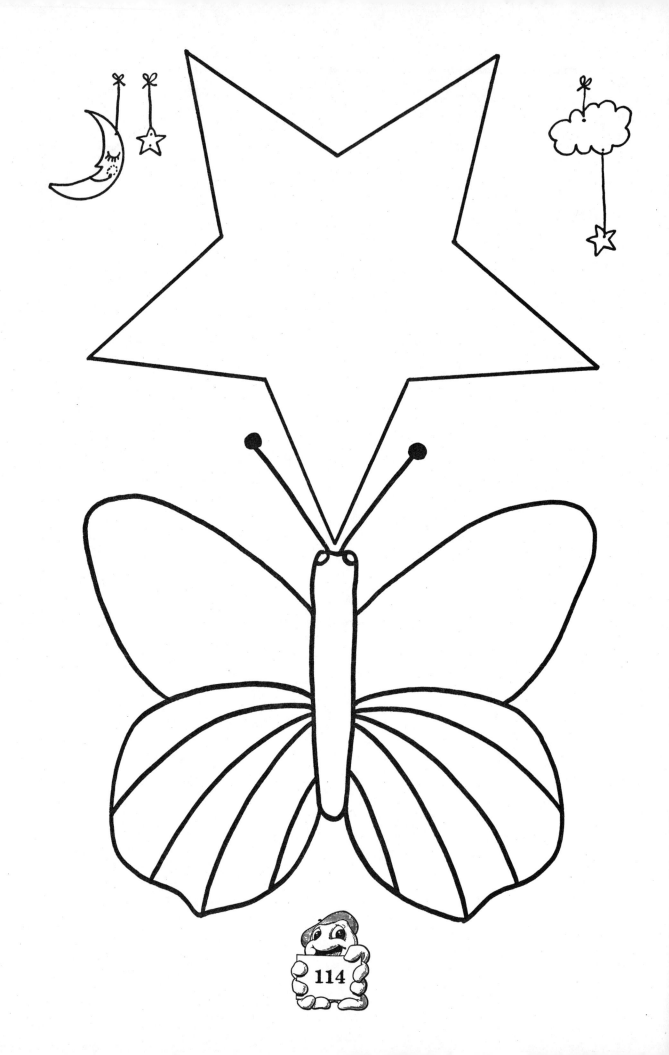

SHAVING

SHAVING SCENE
- Full length mirror
- Waste basket
- Water

SHAVING PROPS
- Hand mirror to look closely
- Paper towels
- Shaving cream
- Tongue depressors

SHAVING CLOTHES
- Shirts

FAST FOOD DINNERS

FAST FOOD SCENE
- Chairs
- Table

FAST FOOD PROPS
- Drink carrier with soda glasses
- Napkins
- Plates
- Several bags of fast food containers
- Silverware

FAST FOOD CLOTHES
- Headbands from restaurants

SHOE SHINE TIME

SHOE SHINE SCENE
- Several pairs of different shoes
- Shoe trees
- Table

SHOE SHINE PROPS
- Empty polish containers
- Newspapers to polish on
- Polishing brushes
- Polish cloths

SHOE SHINE CLOTHES
- Old shirts

WASHING FURNITURE

WASHING FURNITURE SCENE
- Housekeeping furniture
- Tub of rinse water (1/4 full)
- Tub of slightly soapy water (1/4 full)

WASHING FURNITURE PROPS
- Empty spray bottle of polish
- Mop to keep floor dry
- Paper towels
- Polishing cloths
- Sponges
- Towels

WASHING FURNITURE CLOTHES
- Aprons
- Old shirts

PLANTING

PLANTING SCENE
- Table

PLANTING PROPS
- Cups
- Dirt
- Seeds
- Small spoons/shovels
- Sprinkling can
- Tray

PLANTING CLOTHES
- Gardening gloves
- T-Shirts

NEW BABY

NEW BABY SCENE
- Baby dolls
- Buggy
- Crib or cradle
- Rocking chair

NEW BABY PROPS
- Baby magazines
- Bottle
- Music box
- Rattle

NEW BABY CLOTHES
- Baby clothes
- Baby hat
- Blanket

WEDDING

WEDDING SCENE
- Full length mirror
- Table

WEDDING PROPS
- Flowers
- Rings

WEDDING CLOTHES
- Bracelets
- Heels
- Men's coats
- Several fancy dresses
- Ties
- Veils

BIRTHDAY PARTY

BIRTHDAY PARTY SCENE
- Balloons and streamers hanging from ceiling
- Chairs
- Games, like "Pin The Tail On The Donkey"
- Table

BIRTHDAY PARTY PROPS
- Birthday plates, napkins
- Gifts in boxes - top comes off, gift inside
- Pieces of cake
- Spoons
- Tablecloth

BIRTHDAY PARTY CLOTHES
- Hats or crowns

Outside

TAKE CARE OF THE GARDENS: Water the trees, flowers, and plants while they are blooming.

SWEEP THE WALKS: Take several brooms outside. Let the children take turns sweeping the sidewalks and play areas. Be sure to sweep all of the sand back into the sandbox.

TAKE THE BABIES FOR A WALK: Bring the dolls and stuffed animals outside. Let them sit in the shade and watch the children play. Just before going back inside put the dolls in wagons and strollers and take them for a slow walk around the neighborhood.

... *notes for myself* ~

ADDITIONAL RESOURCES

- **Creative Curriculum,** *Dodge.* Seven learning centers including housekeeping.

121

Language

Helps Children With:

Acquaintance With Symbols
Comprehension
Conversation
Listening
Memory
Reading
Visual Discrimination
Writing

Language
Supply List

Equipment

Books
Book Shelf
Chalk Board
Doll House
Felt Board
Magnet Board
Puppet Stage
Record Player
Rocking Chair
Tape Recorder
Write and Wipe Boards

Clean-Up

Broom
Dust Cloth
Dustpan
Erasers
Sponges
Wiping Cloths

Accessories

Alphabet Chart
Blank Books
Carpet Squares
Catalogues
Chalk
Crayons
Erasers
Felt
Felt Letters
Gloves
Magazines
Magnet Letters
Markers
Masonite
Microphone
Notebooks
Paper

Pencils
Pillows
Posterboard
Posters
Puppets
Puzzles
Resonator Blocks
Sand Paper Letters
Scrapbook
Stamp Sets
Stamp Pads
Stencils
Tapes
Telephones
Trays (all sizes)
Tongue Depressors
Wooden Spoons

Felt/Magnet Board

MAKE A SIMPLE FELT BOARD: Get a piece of plywood or heavy-duty corrugated cardboard. Cut it the size you want your felt board to be. Buy a piece of felt to cover both sides of the board. Wrap the felt around the board and securely tape, glue, or staple it to the backside.

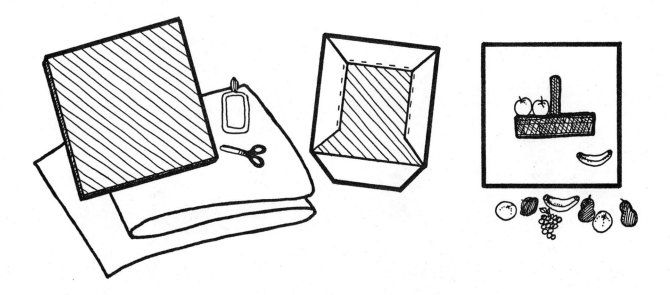

MAKE A FOUR-IN-ONE BOARD: Get a large, sturdy cardboard box from the grocery store. Tape the top and bottom closed. Cover the four remaining sides of the box with felt.

SAY A RHYME: Teach the children rhymes and fingerplays which can be enhanced by easy-to-make felt/magnet pieces. Make the pieces, put them on your felt board, and let the children move them around as they say the rhymes.

TWO LITTLE BLACKBIRDS

Two little black birds sitting on a hill.
One named Jack, one named Jill.
Fly away Jack, fly away Jill.
Come back Jack, come back Jill.

HERE'S A BALL

Here's a ball
And here's a ball
A great big ball I see.
Shall we count them?
Are you ready?
1, 2, 3.

MISSING ANIMALS

There were ten animals
Now there are nine
Guess which one is not in line.

There were nine animals
Now there are eight
Guess which one is not in line.

Continue until all of the animals are gone.

Dick Wilmes

TELL A STORY TO A FRIEND: Make simple felt/magnet pieces which children can use to tell stories to each other.

- Find old story books which have large pictures. Cut the main pictures out of the book and back them with felt/magnet stripping. Tell the story to the children using the pictures; then put them in the language center with the felt/magnet board for the children to use.

- Make felt/magnet pieces which coordinate with simple story lines such as Brown Bear, Brown Bear What Do You See? by Bill Martin.

- Cut out a variety of large shapes and several children from different colors of felt or construction paper. Let your children use the felt/magnet pieces to create their own stories. For variety make stick puppets.

NAME THAT COLOR: Using the pattern, make a large felt/magnet crayon for every color that your children use. Let them play together, one child putting the crayon on the felt/magnet board and others calling out the name of the color.

EXTENSION: Make felt/magnet shapes for other categories such as numbers, letters, food, etc.

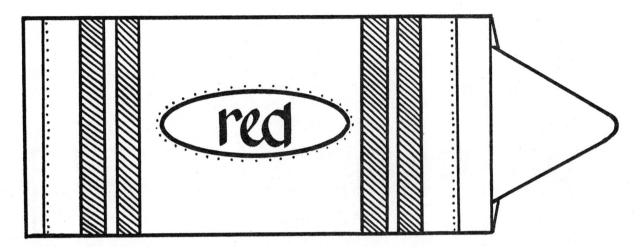

NAMECARD SHOUT: Cut a 3"x6" piece of construction paper for each of the children in your class. Write each child's name on one of the cards. Back each with a piece of felt/magnet stripping. Place all of the namecards in a basket. Put a namecard on the board and read it with the children. Continue until the basket is empty.

SEQUENCE OF EVENTS: Draw or find pictures in books, magazines, and catalogues that show simple sequences of events such as a balloon being blown up, a child dressing, a plant growing, and so on. Back each picture with magnet stripping or felt. Look at the pictures and put them into order.

 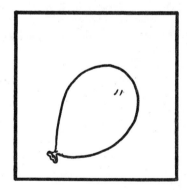 

LARGE TO SMALL: Cut 4-5 felt/magnet triangles ranging in size from large to small. Let the children put them in order. Mix them up and put them in order again, this time beginning with the smallest triangle and going to the largest.

Encourage The Children: *"Portia, show me the smallest triangle." "Karla, am I pointing to the largest triangle or the smallest one?"*

Writing Corner

WRITING TRAYS: Set up different trays so that children can use their fingers to draw letters, designs, messages, scribbles, and squiggles. (Remember that writing is developmental, so that a young child's writing could be a picture or scribble.)

- **Cornstarch Trays:** Mix cornstarch with water or liquid starch until you get a creamy mixture. Put it in a pitcher along with a spoon. Set the pitcher and several small trays on a table. Let the children stir the mixture, pour some onto a tray, and draw.

- **Salt Trays:** Get a large tray. Pour salt on it so that it covers the entire surface. Set it on a table. Let the children draw and write what they choose, then erase it by gently smoothing the salt out with all of their fingers. Draw some more.
  EXTENSION: Add stencils to the tray.

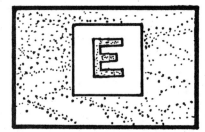

- **Letter Trays:** Get several clear plastic trays and put them on a table. Have large pattern, letter, name, or word cards. Let a child choose a card, put it under the tray, and trace the message with his index finger. Repeat, or remove the card, put it back, and choose a different one.

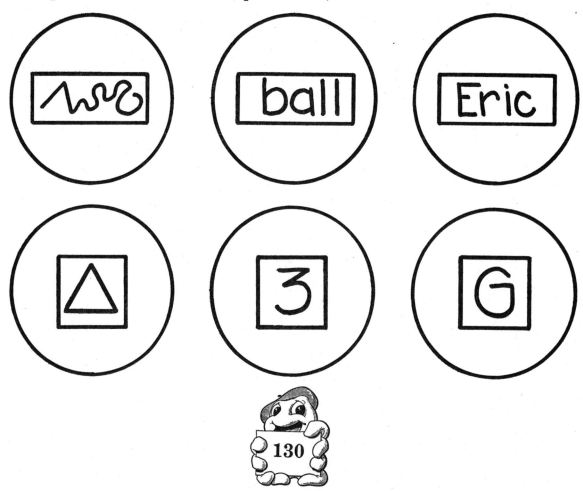

WRITING BOARDS: Set up different types of boards and writing instruments so that children can write and draw letters, designs, messages, scribbles, and squiggles.

- **Write and Wipe Boards:** Put several small write and wipe type boards, special markers, and an eraser on the table. Let children draw, write, erase, and draw some more. Maybe two children would like to work together. Remember to cap the markers.

- **Chalk Boards:** Put several chalk lapboards, along with one or several colors of chalk and erasers on the table.

- **Masonite Boards:** Put several pieces of Masonite, chalk, and a wiping cloth or damp sponge on the table.
Encourage The Children: Have several children write messages or draw pictures and talk about what each did. Maybe each child knows how to "write" his name.

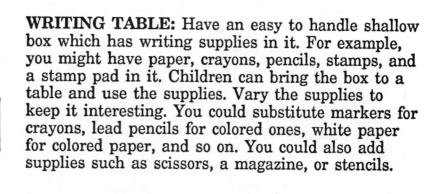

WRITING TABLE: Have an easy to handle shallow box which has writing supplies in it. For example, you might have paper, crayons, pencils, stamps, and a stamp pad in it. Children can bring the box to a table and use the supplies. Vary the supplies to keep it interesting. You could substitute markers for crayons, lead pencils for colored ones, white paper for colored paper, and so on. You could also add supplies such as scissors, a magazine, or stencils.

LINKING THOUGHTS: Cut 2"x6" strips of white construction paper. Choose a topic such as things that are white, types of furniture, body parts, things you are thankful for, people you love, and so on. Say to the children, *"Let's name all of the things we can think of that are white. When you name one, I'll write it on one of these strips of paper."* Have the children start naming things while you write each one down on a strip.

   After you have made the strips, link them together in a teardrop chain with the words on the outside. As you and the children make your chain, read the words to them. Let the children decide where to hang it.
EXTENSION: Choose other topics and link their thoughts together again and again.

COPY CAT BOOKS: Make a series of Copy Cat books for children to write in. Make each book as follows.

FRONT-BACK COVERS

- Cut 2, 7"x9" rectangles from your piece of colored posterboard. Trace the cat pattern on each piece, add facial features to one cat for the front cover and a tail to the other one for the back cover, and cut them out.

PAGES

- Trace and cut out as many cat pages as you need for each book.
- Divide each page vertically in half.
- On the left half of each page, draw the line or pattern you want the children to copy.
- Punch holes near the ears in the covers and pages.
- Laminate the pages and covers, re-punch the holes, and clip them together with a large metal ring.

TO USE: Have a child chose the Copy Cat book he wants to write in, get his washable markers, and open the book to the first page. Have him look at the marking on the left side and copy it in the empty space. Continue through the entire book. After he is finished, have him take a cloth and erase all of his markings so that the book is ready for another child.

POSSIBLE COPY CAT BOOKS:

8-10 pages
Large colored
squiggles to
copy

26 pages
Upper or
lower case
letters to copy

Any number
of pages

Shapes to
copy

Any number
of pages

Letters in the
center to
trace with
your index
finger

Any number
of pages
Numerals to
copy

Any number
of pages
Designs to
copy

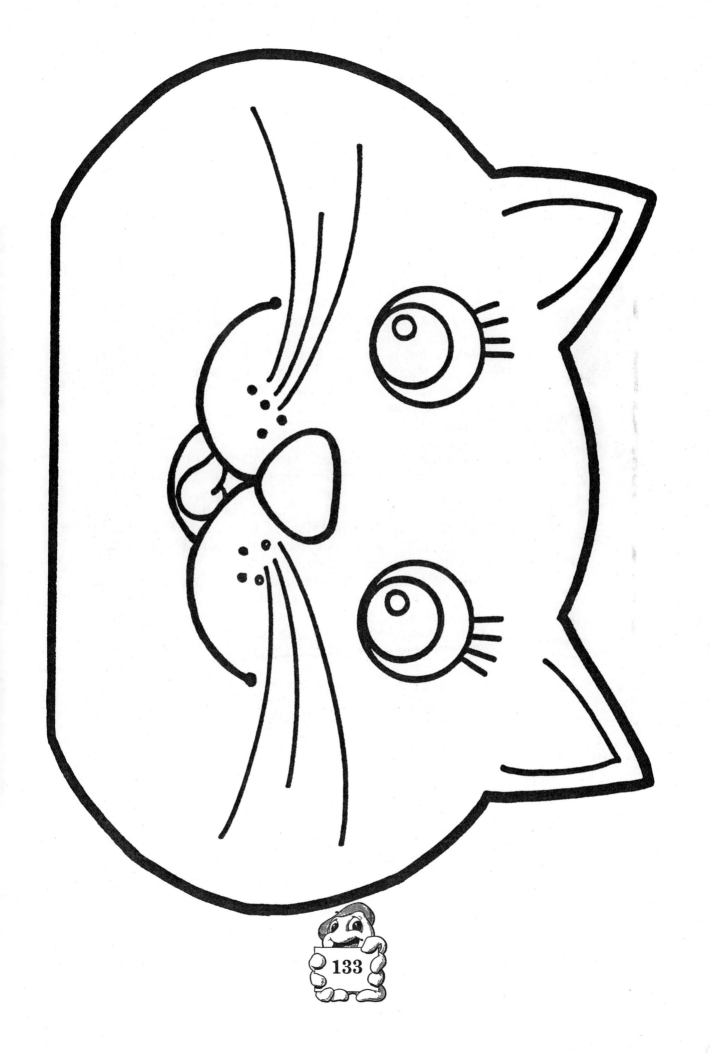

DICTATE AND WRITE: Make simple books with the children. They may be books which the whole group has put together, a small group has dictated, or an individual has thought about and dictated or written.

- **Children's Journals:** Have simple notebooks with plain white pages in them. Let each child help you write his name on his notebook. Have him draw a picture or design on the front cover if he would like.

  Put the journals on a shelf which the children can easily reach. When a child wants to 'write' or draw in his book, he can get it, and jot down his thoughts. If possible use parent volunteers to write children's dictations in their books.

- **Photo Book:** Take advantage of field trips and special activities to put group books together. While enjoying the trip/activity take a series of photographs. Glue the photographs to pieces of posterboard. Put them in order. Show each one to the children. Let them say something about each photo. Write what they say below each picture. Add a front/back cover. Punch holes in the sides of the covers and pages and loosely put them together with brightly colored yarn or metal rings.

- **Shape Book:** From posterboard, cut a front/back cover and pages to identify a specific shape such as a circle. Have several magazines and catalogues, scissors, and paste. Put all of the supplies on a table. Sit with the children and look through the magazines/catalogues for pictures with circles in them. Cut the pictures out and paste them to the circle pages. Add children's dictations to the pages.

  Punch a hole near the top of each circle and link the pages together with yarn or a metal ring. Keep adding pages as time goes on and children find more pictures. If the children are really interested in shapes they could work on several different books at the same time.

- **Ongoing Story:** Cut 9"x12" front/back covers from posterboard. Use posterboard/construction paper pages. Punch three holes in the covers and pages and link them together with metal rings. Show the children the empty book and tell them that over the next several weeks they are going to all help write a book.

  You start the story, by saying and writing something like *"Rig was a dog who lived with Sergio and Junior. He was big and loved to play."* Then say to the children that you want them to think of adventures that they might do with Rig. Each day brainstorm one of the children's adventures. Write down what they say on pages of the book. Every couple of days read the story to the children. When the book is finished, send it home on a rotating basis for each child to share with his family.

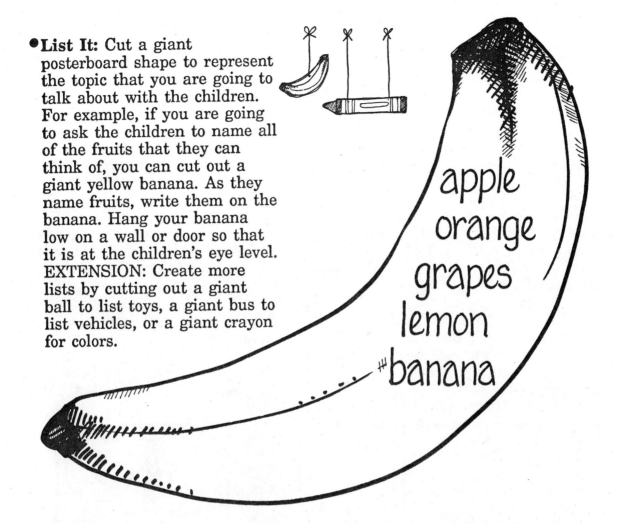

●**List It:** Cut a giant posterboard shape to represent the topic that you are going to talk about with the children. For example, if you are going to ask the children to name all of the fruits that they can think of, you can cut out a giant yellow banana. As they name fruits, write them on the banana. Hang your banana low on a wall or door so that it is at the children's eye level. EXTENSION: Create more lists by cutting out a giant ball to list toys, a giant bus to list vehicles, or a giant crayon for colors.

apple
orange
grapes
lemon
banana

●**Here We Are:** Get a large scrapbook with plain pages. On each page trace the children's hands and write their names. Over the next several weeks take time to let each child draw designs and pictures on his page. Then ask him if he would like to tell about himself and you will write what he says on his page. After the book is finished, read it to the children. Put it on the book shelf for the children to enjoy over and over again. Set it on a table for parents to read during an open house or family party.

Children could talk about their:
    Favorite foods
    What they like to play
    Their families
    Their pets
    Favorite T.V. shows
    What they like to do at home
    Where they like to go

Posters

SIGN LANGUAGE: Hang posters at the children's eye level which show the sign language alphabet, simple signing, and rhymes written in sign language. Duplicate the song on the following page, teach it to your children, and hang it up so they can sing and sign often.

OCCUPATION POSTERS: Call your local police and fire departments, hospitals, traffic departments, road construction office, etc. and see if they have some community helper posters which they could give you for your room. Hang them up one or two at a time.

Encourage The Children: Talk with the children about the different uniforms or work clothes each person is wearing. Is the worker wearing any special safety clothing such as a hard hat or glasses? What do the children think the workers do at their jobs? Has the worker ever helped the children or their families? How?

INFORMATION POSTERS: Get posters which picture foods, animals, safety, and so on. Use the pictures to help children begin to understand different concepts and habits. For example, hang a *Buckle-Up For Safety* poster and talk about how to use seat belts in cars and buses. Duplicate the food poster below. Glue it to a piece of colored paper. Use it to talk about different foods the children should eat each day.

AESTHETIC POSTERS: Find posters that are simply pleasing and restful to look at. Hang one or two.

THE MORE WE GET TOGETHER

(Tune: Did You Ever See a Lassie)

The more we get together, together, together,

the more we get together the happier we'll be,

'cause your friends are my friends

and my friends are your friends

The more we get together, the happier we'll be.

Encourage Listening

LISTENING BOX: Get a small box with a lid, such as one for shoes or boots. Wrap the box and lid with a patterned adhesive paper. Put an object in the box. Cover the box and tie it closed with a brightly colored yarn.

Have the children shake it, roll it, rock it, and so on, to see if they can figure out what is in the box by listening to the sounds that the object makes. After the children have had a chance to listen to it and talk about their ideas, open the box and see what the object is.

EXTENSION: Put one, two, or three of the same object/s in the box, such as two marbles, bells, or erasers. Let the children listen carefully and see if they can determine what the object is and how many objects are in the box.

TAPES AND RECORDS: Set up a small listening area in your language center. Have several large pillows or rocking chairs along with a record player and/or tape recorder plus headphones. Have a wide variety of different stories, music, rhymes, and songs available for the children to listen to. (Make your own tapes or check them out of your local library.)

WHISPER TIME: Have a large sign which you can put at the entrance to the language center, indicating that while in the area, everyone must whisper. This sign can be posted for an entire day, a short time, once a week, or whatever seems to be appropriate for your group of children.

CUDDLE UP AND READ: Have an adult size rocking chair in the center. Ask volunteers (or do it yourself when you have extra moments) to read to children one at a time. An adult can sit in the chair with a child next to him/her on his/her lap.

RESONATOR BLOCKS: Have a set of resonator blocks. Encourage the children to really listen to the sounds which the different blocks make when tapped with a mallet. For example put the resonator tray on the table with only two blocks. Tap one - listen. Tap the second one - listen. Which sound does the child like better? Which one sounds louder? Continue throughout the year mixing and matching the blocks and listening to the sounds.

Encourage Talking

TO YOURSELF: Set up different activities which would encourage children to talk to themselves or pretend to be talking to others.

- **Microphones:** Put one microphone on the shelf. Children can hold it and pretend to be singing to large groups, announcing a special message, telling a story, chattering to friends, and so on.

- **Mitten Puppets:** Get a mitten. Put one side of a velcro dot on the thumb of the mitten and one dot on the finger section. Make two simple faces. Put the other halves of the velcro dots on the backsides of the faces. Attach the faces to the mitten. A child can slip the mitten on and let the two people talk to each other or maybe tell each other favorite stories.
  VARIATION: Instead of having two faces on the mitten, have a face and an animal, two animals, or a child with a specific person such as a mom.

TWO PEOPLE: Set up activities which would encourage two people to talk to each other.

- **Walkie-Talkies:** Cut 2, 3"x6" pieces of thick corrugated cardboard or styrofoam. Using a permanent marker, draw simple controls on each piece. Stick a pipe cleaner or straw into the top of each walkie-talkie for the antenna. Set the walkie-talkies on the language shelf or window ledge. Let two children talk to each other over their walkie-talkies. *"10-4, Good buddy!"*

- **Telephones:** Set two telephones on the top of your language shelf or make your own telephones. Get two toilet paper rolls and a 5-6 foot piece of yarn. Punch one hole in each roll. Tie the two rolls together so that they are attached with 4-5 feet between them. Set the rolls on the shelf. Let the children call each other; you call a child; you call another adult.

- **Megaphones:** Get several megaphones or make your own by rolling lightweight cardboard into cone shapes. Set them in the language area and encourage two people to talk.

SMALL GROUPS: Set up activities which encourage several children to talk with each other.

- **Texture Tent:** Get a large appliance box. Cut and fold it into a tent shape. Gather two identical pieces of 8 to 10 types of papers and fabrics which have different textures, (sandpaper, aluminum foil, furry fabric, corrugated cardboard, textured wallpaper, piece of carpeting, and so on). Glue one texture from each pair to the inside of the tent. Glue the duplicate set to the outside of the tent.

  Set the 'Texture Tent' in a quiet place. Secure the edges to the floor with wide tape. Encourage the children to crawl through it, find each texture, and feel it. Talk about the textures. Walk to the outside of the tent and touch each texture again.

  EXTENSION: Glue duplicate sets of objects on the inside and outside of the tent, (rubber bands, pencils, paper cups, pizza boards, bottle caps, paper clips, pom-poms, jar lids, egg cartons, etc.). After another period of time add foot long pieces of different types of string, ribbon, shoe laces, yarn, twine, and rope to the tent. When finished with the 'Texture Tent,' open it up and hang it low on a wall so that the children can see, feel, and talk about the objects one more time. Turn the board around and feel the other side.

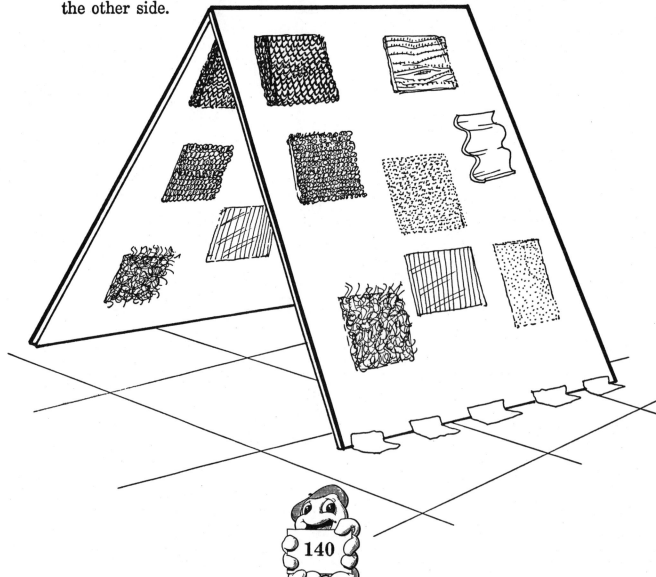

● **Conversation Corner:** Put a small table in a secluded area of the center. When children bring things to school to show the others, have them put the objects on the table. During free choice, children can tell others about the things they have brought in to share.

● **Television:** Get a broken television set and take all of the insides out or make your own by cutting off one side of a large box and cutting a large opening in the opposite side. Set the television on a table. Lay puppets such as the Sesame Street characters, near the set. Put several chairs in front of the set. Several children can produce the television show while others watch.

● **Doll House:** Put a large doll house with people, furniture, and accessories on a table. Let children mix and match all of the pieces as they play.
Encourage The Children: "Shadra, looks like your family is about ready to have dinner. What are they going to eat?" "Caleb, the children are playing outside. Are they going to the park?"

Book Shelf

ROTATING AROUND: Change the books on your shelf often so that there is always a selection of new choices and old favorites.

Tell the children about the new books that you are adding to the shelf and which ones you are taking away for awhile. Read as many books aloud as possible. When deciding what books to put on your shelf, think about the children in your room. What are they interested in? What is happening in their lives? What special topics are you talking about? Do certain children like specific topics? Remember to look for books which depict males and females of different cultures, abilities, ages, and activities.

FEATURED BOOKS: Have a special place on the book shelf to display special books such as:
- A book that a child has brought from home to share.
- A book that a child has written.
- A book that has been written in braille.
- A book that has been written in a foreign language.
- The classroom picture album each time you've added new photographs.

MORE THAN BOOKS: On one level of your book shelf put several magazines, catalogues, and brochures which you think your children would enjoy looking through and talking about.

HAVE A LOOK THROUGH A BOOK: Encourage the children to take a book or magazine off of the book shelf and 'read' it.

- **Carpet Squares:** Have a stack of 4-5 carpet squares near the book shelf. Children can take one and sit/lie on it while enjoying a book.

- **In A Box:** Get several boxes large enough for a child to sit in. Cover them with wallpaper or adhesive paper. Put them near the book shelf. Let the children choose books and 'read' them while sitting in the special boxes.

Puppets

MAKE A STAGE: Make a simple puppet stage for the children to use.

- Get a sturdy medium size box from the grocery store. Cut off the top and one side. On the side opposite the opening, cut out a large window.

- Get a large appliance box. Cut off 2 of the long sides. Cut several windows along one of the other sides. Set the box on the floor. Add puppets. Let the children poke the puppets through the windows to talk to each other and tell stories.

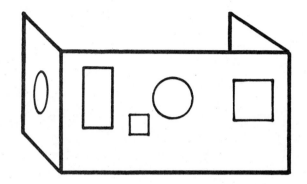

- Simply use the top of a table as a stage. The puppets can walk on it or stand behind it.

- Add accessories to a puppet stage that you've purchased. You could tape different fabrics to the opening to act as a curtain and set three or four puppets on a shelf. For example have a blue fabric and water animal puppets or a brightly striped fabric with clown puppets.

SPOON PUPPETS: Get 3 to 5 large wooden spoons. Using permanent markers draw a feeling face on each one. Let the children use the spoon puppets to identify different feelings, talk about how they feel, and have conversations with each other.

Get a thick piece of styrofoam to stick the handles of the puppets into. Set the puppets on a shelf or window ledge.

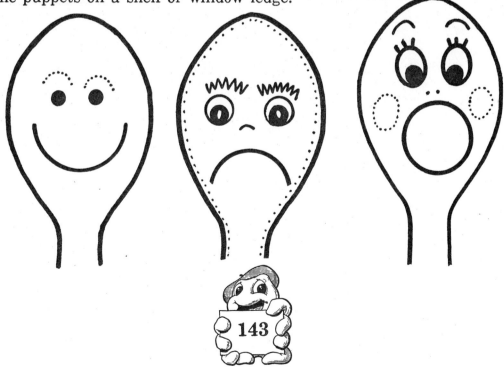

GLOVE PUPPETS: Teach your children fingerplays, rhymes, and songs which are easily enhanced by one or two gloves. Once they are familiar with the words, put the puppets in the language area. A cup holder laying on its backside makes a perfect puppet rack.

WHERE IS THUMBKIN?

Where is Thumbkin? Where is Thumbkin?
Here I am. Here I am.
How are you today sir?
Very well I thank you.
Run away. Run away.

Where is pointer? Where is pointer?

Where is tall man? Where is tall man?

Where is ring man? Where is ring man?

Where is baby? Where is baby?

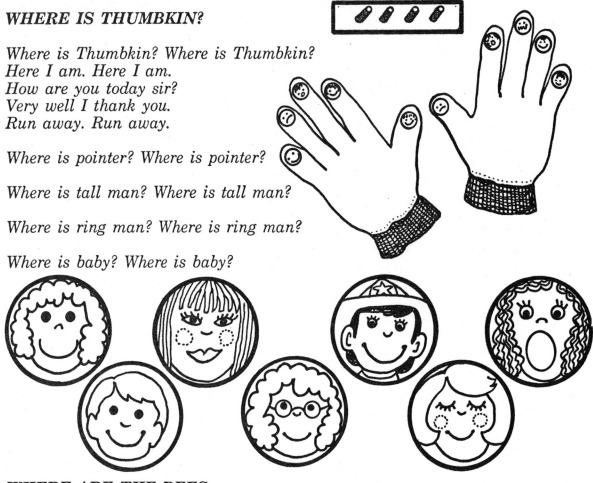

WHERE ARE THE BEES

Where are the bees?
Hidden away where nobody sees.
Here they come creeping out of the hive.
1, 2, 3, 4, 5.

144

STICK PUPPETS: Use the patterns and tongue depressors to make a series of farm animal stick puppets. Let the children use the puppets to tell stories to each other, take imaginary trips to the farm, and enhance rhymes and songs.

String a short piece of heavy twine in the language area. Clip each puppet to the twine with a clothespin. Children can easily see the puppets and reach the ones they want.

WALKING FINGER PUPPETS: Use posterboard and the patterns to make a series of community helper walking finger puppets. Show the children how to put their fingers through the holes and walk their puppets. Encourage them to talk about how each person helps them, what they do on their jobs, and so on.

Cut a 8"x22" piece of posterboard. Slip 5-6 large plastic paper clips along the edge. Slip one puppet into each paper clip. Set the puppets on the top of a cabinet.

SIMPLY USE YOUR FINGER: Add a simple drawing or design to your finger and make it talk.

- **Draw A Face:** Using a ballpoint pen, draw a face on your two pointer fingers. Let them talk to each other or find more friends to talk with.

- **Stickers:** Have a variety of small stickers available. Let a child choose one to wear on his finger. It can be his buddy for as long as he wants. When he's finished, he can save it on the back of his hand. When the child wants his puppet to return, he can simply put it back on his finger.

- **Fabric Fun:** Cut heavy-duty fabric such as felt or denim into triangles. Children can wrap the fabric around their fingers and pretend that it is a face, a hat, a scarf, etc. For example, cut a red felt triangle, wrap it around your pointer finger, and tell someone the story of Little Red Riding Hood. Have several children put on their hats, and talk about what they do in the snow.

- **Glove It:** Cut the fingers off of old gloves. Draw faces on the fingers. Choose which one you want to talk to, slip it on a finger, and have a great discussion.

- **Color Dots:** Using washable markers draw big dots of color on one or more of each child's fingers. Throughout the day let the colors talk to each other.
Encourage The Children: "Hi, I'm Red. Who are you?" "You're sure colorful. Bow your red finger please."

- **Number Nonsense:** On one set of each child's fingers write the numerals 1-5. On the other hand write 6-10. Let the children enjoy rhymes, name numbers, match fingers, etc.
Encourage The Children: "I'm waving number 3 at you. Wave a number back."

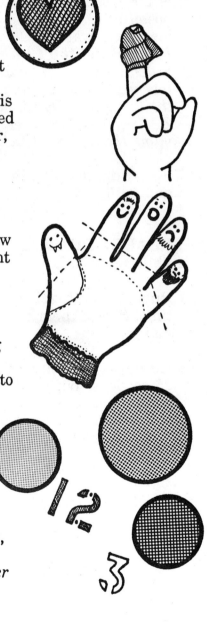

147

Alphabet Games

TOUCHING LETTERS: Set up alphabet activities in which children cannot only see all of the letters, but can easily touch them.

● **Lacing Letters:** Cut out a set of large posterboard letters. Punch holes along each one. Cut out 26 one-foot pieces of yarn. Put tape around one end of each piece to form a point. Tape each needle to one end of a letter. Set the 'Lacing Letters' on a tray.

● **Sandpaper Letter Chart:** Get a piece of posterboard and coarse sandpaper. Cut out a set of large sandpaper letters. Glue the letters to the posterboard. Hang the chart at children's eye level on a wall.

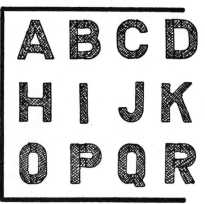

Encourage The Children: "Lluvia, I've been watching you. You started with the letter 'A' and touched the whole alphabet. Now you're feeling the last letter. Do you know its name? Its called Z." "Vanessa, can I feel the letters with you? Let's name them as we touch them."

● **Felt/Magnet Letters:** Cut out a set of felt/magnet letters. Put the letters and felt/magnet board out for the children to use.

ALPHABET PUZZLES: Set different types of alphabet puzzles on your shelf for children to use.

● **Purchased Puzzles:** Offer one or two commercial alphabet puzzles at a time. Rotate them every several weeks so that children have fresh materials.

● **Alphabet Worm:** Cut a long, fat worm out of posterboard. Divide it into 26 sections. Write a letter in each section. Cut the worm into as many puzzle pieces as you think would be appropriate for your children. Put the pieces in a resealable bag. Let the children put the puzzle together on the floor or table.

Alpha Bee: Cut out 26 posterboard bees with only one wing. Cut 26 wings. In each wing attached to a bee, write an upper case letter. In each separate wing write a lower case letter. Put all of the bees and wings on a tray and let the children pair them.

Alphabet Balls: Using the patterns on the next four pages, make 26 alphabet balls. To make them cut out 26, 3" posterboard circles. Duplicate the patterns, color them, cut them out, and glue them to the posterboard circles. Laminate or cover each one with clear adhesive paper. Using a variety of cut lines, cut each circle in two pieces, so that the upper case letter is on one part and the lower case letter is on the other part.

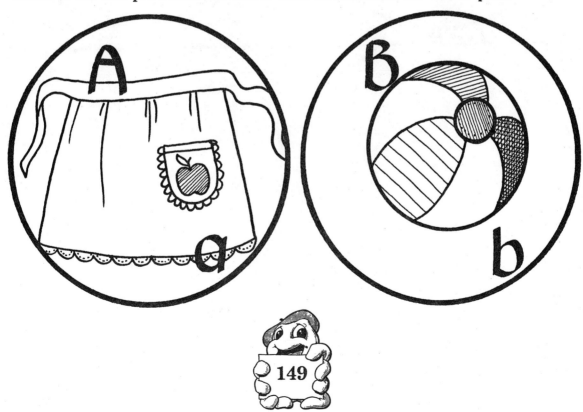

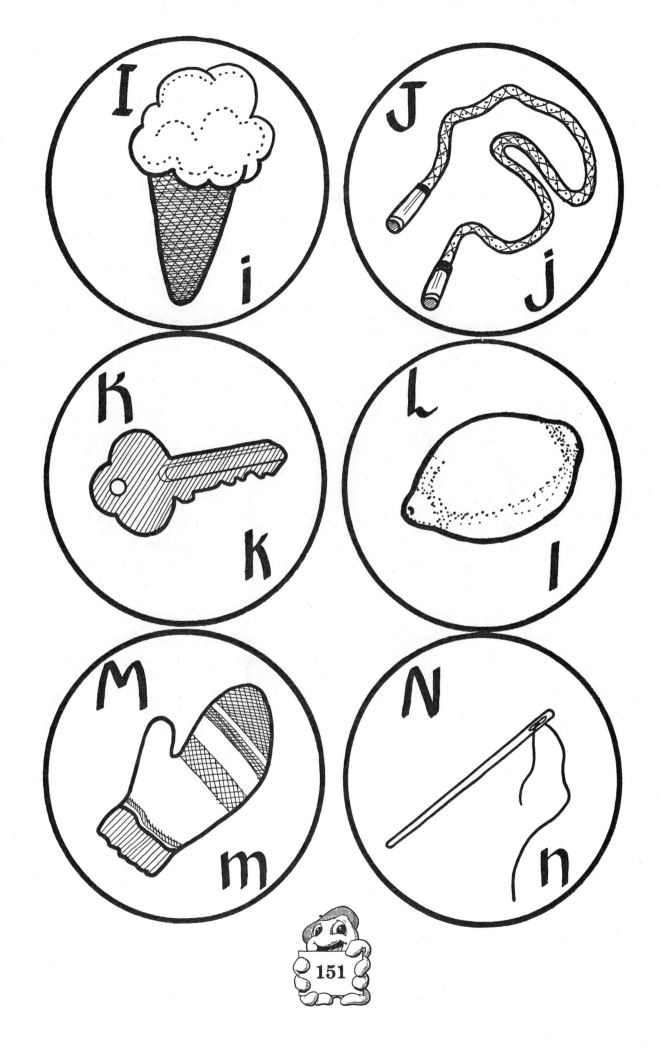

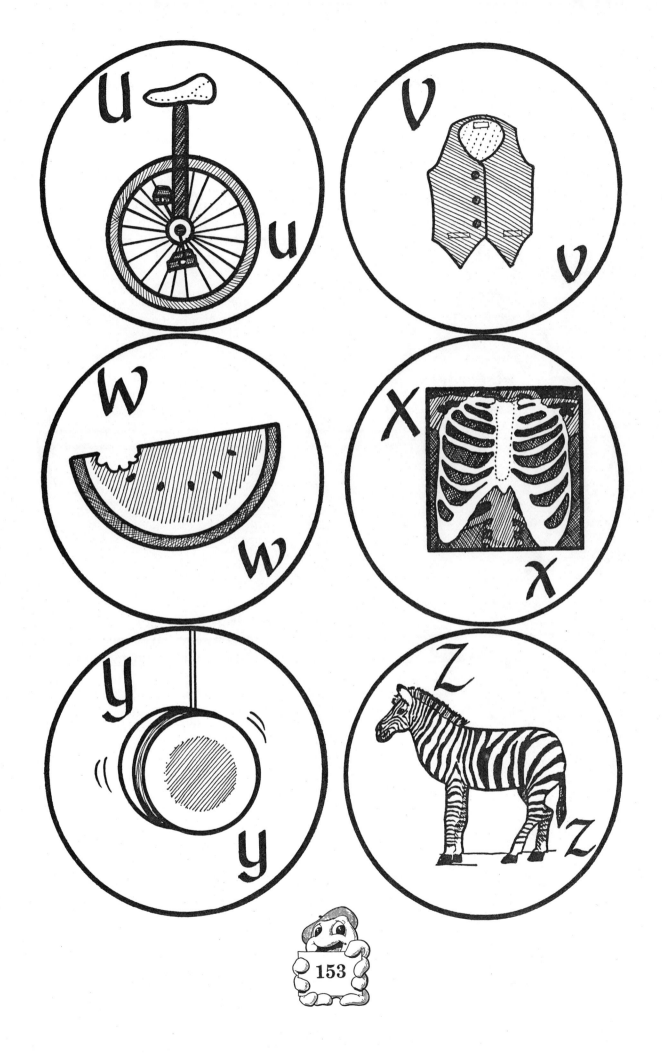

NAMING AND RECOGNIZING LETTERS: Set up activities to help the children name the letters and discriminate among them.

- **ABC Chart:** Duplicate the alphabet chart on the next page. Glue it to a piece of colored construction paper. Hang it at the children's eye level on a wall, door, or cabinet.

- **Key Letters:** Using the pattern make 26 large posterboard keys. Punch a hole in the top of each one. Write a letter on each key. Link them together on a giant key ring. Sit with children and talk about the letters on the different keys. Take them off of the ring, mix them up, and alphabetize them.

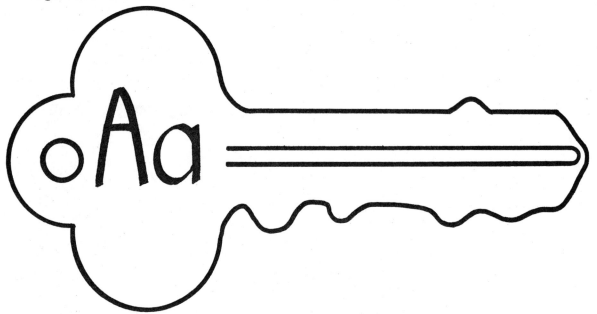

- **Alphabet Headbands:** Make headbands for all of the letters. Set all or a few on a shelf. Children can wear them as they choose.
  Encourage The Children: *"Betty, you're wearing an alphabet headband. Which one did you choose?" "Joe, look at Greg. He is wearing the 'G' headband."*

- **Alphabet Hunt:** Get a special box like a Valentine candy box. Make lots of letter cards along with cards which have miscellaneous pictures on them. Before the children come, hide all of the cards. Tell the children that you have hidden lots of cards all over the room. Some of the cards have letters on them and some have only pictures. As the children are playing they should look for the cards with letters on them. When they find a card, pick it up, and put it in the special box. (Show them.) Throughout the hunt name the letters which the children have found.

Aa Bb Cc Dd

Ee Ff Gg Hh

Ii Jj Kk Ll

Mm Nn Oo Pp

Qq Rr Ss Tt

Uu Vv Ww Xx

Yy Zz

155

Outside

LOOK AND LIST: Cut out a large posterboard cloud. Take it outside with a marker. Put the cloud and marker on a table. As the children are playing, have them look up at the sky. When anyone sees something he should tell you what it is. You write it on the cloud.

Take the list inside, and punch a hole in it, lace twine through the hole and hang it from the ceiling. Within the next several weeks, cut out a large posterboard bus. Take a walk to a parking lot or sit on a sidewalk and look at all of the vehicles. Let the children call out the different ones they see while you write them down. Continue the activity every couple weeks or so with a new shape.

airplane
kite
sun

trunk
bark
leaves
ants
birds

bus
trailer   truck
jeep

... notes for myself ~

ADDITIONAL RESOURCES

- **Circle Time,** *Wilmes/Wilmes.* Language activities, fingerplays and more for 39 holidays/seasons.
- **Everyday Circle Times,** *Wilmes/Wilmes.* Language activities, fingerplays and more for 48 themes including animals, five senses, and more.
- **Felt Board Fun,** *Wilmes/Wilmes.* 150 activities plus patterns.
- **Imagination Stretchers,** *Wilmes/Wilmes.* Language starters for creative discussions, simple lists, beginning dictations, and writings.
- **Make-Take Games,** *Wilmes/Wilmes.* Instructions and illustrations to make 32 games.
- **Make-Take Games Companion Pattern Set.** Full-size patterns (animals, foods, people, leaves, etc.) to make the 32 games. Easily adapted for other language activities.
- **Mitt Magic,** *Roberts.* Fingerplays with accompanying finger puppet patterns.
- **More Story Stretchers,** *Raines/Canady.* Activities to accompany 90 more young children's favorite books.
- **1,2,3 Puppets,** *Warren.* 50 simple puppets with patterns and original song or rhyme.
- **Puppetry In Early Childhood Education,** *Hunt/Renfro.* Easy-to-make puppets with accompanying patterns and lots of activities.
- **Ring A Ring O'Roses.** Fingerplay book.
- **Signs For Me,** *Bahan/Dannis.* Easy sign language book for common words used by young children.
- **Story Stretchers,** *Raines/Canady.* Activities to expand 90 favorite children's books.
- **Yearful of Circle Times,** *Wilmes/Wilmes.* Language activities, fingerplays, and more for 52 different themes to use throughout the year.

Large Motor

Helps Children With:

Balance
Cooperative Play
Exercise
Flexibility
Motor Control
Movements
Safety
Strength

Large Motor
Supply List

Equipment

Balance Beam
Climber
Flat Ladder
Giant Saucers
Parachute
Record Player
Riding Toys
Rocking Boat
Scooter Board
Sled
Slides
Stairs
Tape Recorder
Tires
Tumbling Mat
Tunnels
Wheelbarrow
Woodworking Bench

Clean-Up

Door Mat
Large Containers for
   Accessories
Shelving Units With
   Labeled Shelves
Soap
Sponges
Water

Accessories

Balls
Beanbags
Flags
Exercise Charts
Frisbees
Full Length Mirror
Garden Tools
Hoops
Musical Tapes
Posters
Records
Rhythm Instruments
Rakes
Ropes
Safety Goggles
Scarves
Snow Shovels
Streamers
Tape
Targets
Traffic Cones
Traffic Signs
Wading Pool
Woodworking Tools

160

Active Rhymes

RHYME POSTERS: Duplicate each rhyme and glue it to a piece of colored construction paper. Hang one poster at a time at the children's eye level. Teach the children the rhyme and then encourage them to enjoy it on their own.

JOHNNY WORKS WITH ONE HAMMER

Johnny works with one hammer
(Pound with one fist.)
One hammer, one hammer,
Johnny works with one hammer
Now he works with two.

Johnny works with two hammers
(Pound both fists.)
Two hammers, two hammers,
Johnny works with two hammers
Now he works with three.

Johnny works with three hammers
(Pound two fists and one leg.)
Three hammers, three hammers,
Johnny works with three hammers
Now he works with four.

Johnny works with four hammers
(Pound two fists and two legs.)
Four hammers, four hammers,
Johnny works with four hammers
Now he works with five.

Johnny works with five hammers
(Pound two fists & legs, and head)
Five hammers, five hammers,
Johnny works with five hammers
Now he goes to sleep.
(Lie down.)

BEAR HUNT

Let's go on a bear hunt.
OK, let's go.
Open the door, walk outside.
Lock the door, put the key in your pocket.
Walk down to the sidewalk.
Thump, thump, thump.

(Slap thighs and pretend to walk.)

Oh look! I see a tree.
Can't go around it.
Can't go under it.
Let's climb up it. (Climb with arms)
OK let's go.
Climb, climb, climb. (Slap thighs.)

Oh look! I see a swamp.
Can't go around it.
Can't go under it.
Let's swim through it. (Swim)
OK let's go.
Swim, swim, swim. (Slap thighs.)

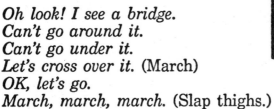

Oh look! I see a bridge.
Can't go around it.
Can't go under it.
Let's cross over it. (March)
OK, let's go.
March, march, march. (Slap thighs.)

Oh look! I see a cave.
Can't go around it.
Can't go through it.
Let's crawl into it. (Crawl in place)
OK, let's go.
Crawl, crawl, crawl. (Slap thighs.)

Gee -- its dark in here.
Better get out my flashlight.
Doesn't work.
I think I see something.
It's BIG! It's FURRY! It's got a BIG NOSE!
I think it's a BEAR!   IT IS A BEAR!!!
Let's get out of here!!!!!

Say the stanzas in reverse order
until you are safely back home.

THE WHEELS ON THE BUS

The wheels on the bus go round and round,
Round and round, round and round.
The wheels on the bus go round and round,
All through the town.

The people on the bus go up and down,
Up and down, up and down.
The people on the bus go up and down,
All through the town.

The money on the bus goes clink, clink, clink,
Clink, clink, clink; clink, clink, clink.
The money on the bus goes clink, clink, clink,
All through the town.

The driver on the bus says, "Move on back," etc.

The children on the bus say, "Yak, yak, yak," etc.

The babies on the bus say, "Waa, waa, waa," etc.

The parents on the bus say, "Sh, sh, sh," etc.

The wipers on the bus go swish, swish, swish, etc.

The horn on the bus goes honk, honk, honk, etc.

The door on the bus goes open and shut, open and shut, etc.

The wheels on the bus go round and round,
Round and round, round and round.
The wheels on the bus go round and round,
All through the town.

Balance Beam

WALK THE BALANCE BEAM:
Duplicate the 'Balance Beam Warm-Up Chart' and glue it to a piece of colored construction paper. Hang it near your balance beam. Have the children limber up by doing the movements pictured and then try their own favorites or new ones they've just created.

Encourage The Children: Have a container of beanbags, clothespins, or small blocks near the beam. Suggest that children balance one or more on their arm, shoulder, or palm as they move down the beam.

OBSTACLE COURSE: Have a container of colored clothespins near the beam. Before a child moves down the beam, have him place several clothespins along the board. When he gets to each obstacle, he can avoid it in a variety of ways: walk over it; get off, walk around it, and get back on; bend down and pick it up; or gently kick it off. Continue avoiding obstacles until you reach the end of the beam.

Balls

BOUNCING BALLS: With a piece of colored tape, mark off a 3'x5' area of the floor next to an empty wall. Have a playground ball available and let the children do ball activities in the space:

- Hold the ball with two hands, bounce it on the floor, and catch it. Repeat as often as desired.

- Bounce the ball on the floor with one hand.

- One child stands at each end of the space. Have the children bounce the ball back and forth to each other.

- Sit in the space. Roll the ball at the wall and have the child catch it as it comes back to him.

- Stand on the line, bounce the ball at the wall, and catch it again.

- Have children create more activities.

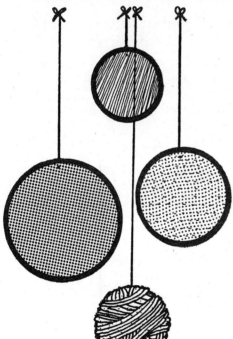

YARN BALL SWAT: Set up a simple target by hanging 3 or 4 large different colored posterboard circles from the ceiling. Hang a yarn ball within the children's reach near the colored targets. The children can reach up and swat the yarn ball at any of the targets. *Encourage The Children: Ask the children if they noticed which colored target they hit. You could give directions such as, "Elizabeth, see if you can hit the blue circle."*

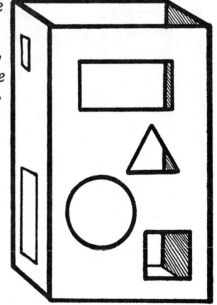

BALL TOSS: Get a large sturdy box or rubber waste basket. Cut several large holes in the sides. Put 6-8 tennis balls in it. Have children stand away from the basket and toss the balls through the holes you cut out or simply into the top. Fetch the balls and toss again.

Beanbags

SHOE IT: Get a large sturdy box and cut off the top. Cut different size notches along the four sides. Turn the box over so that the openings are on

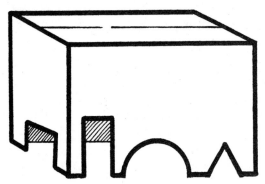

the floor. Have lots of beanbags. Kneel away from the box and slide the beanbags towards the box, trying to get them through the openings. Get the ones that missed and slide them again.
Encourage The Children: *"Bryant, go get the red beanbags and slide them into the box. Give me one to try."*

BEANBAG SHUFFLE BOARD: Get a large appliance box. Cut off one side of it. On the blank side of the piece you cut, draw a variety of large shapes with a wide black marker. Put the board on the floor. Have a child-size broom or two and lots of beanbags.

Put all of the beanbags on the edge of the board. Sweep them down the board trying to land on the different shapes. Talk about where your beanbags stopped.
VARIATION: Instead of drawing various shapes, draw different colored circles, write numerals or letters, or draw different sizes of the same shape. For holidays and seasons use an easily recognizable symbol such as pumpkins for fall or snowmen for winter.

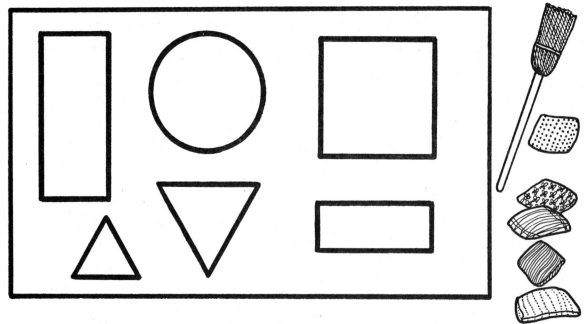

FEED THE CLOWN: Get a tall, light-colored, rubber waste basket. Using permanent markers draw a clown face with a huge mouth on it. Carefully cut out the mouth. Have children stand away from the basket and toss beanbags into the mouth. Get the ones that missed and toss again.

BEANBAG BALANCE: Put a container of beanbags on the shelf. Have children put them on different parts of their bodies (heads, shoulders, foreheads, chests, feet, etc.) and balance them as they walk around.
Encourage The Children: "Mark you're balancing your beanbags so carefully on your shoulders." Give a beanbag to a child and have him put it someplace on his body and then ask him to walk to a certain place and back again.

BEANBAG TOSS: Put a hoop on the floor. Stand away from the hoop and toss beanbags into it.

Exercise Chart

BEND AND STRETCH: Duplicate the 'Bend and Stretch Chart' and hang it at children's eye level in the large motor area. Place the full length mirror near the chart. Have children look at the chart and exercise in place along with Teddy Bear. They can watch themselves moving in the mirror.
Encourage The Children: *"Caesar, you're legs are really moving!" "Maki, you're bending up and down just like Mr. Bear."*

TEDDY SAYS, EXERCISE: Duplicate Teddy Bear doing each of his exercises. (Enlarge them if you would like.) Cut each one out and glue it to a piece of colored construction paper. Hang one exercise at children's eye level in the large motor area. Tell the children which exercise Teddy has chosen for them to do that day. Change the exercise every day or so.
Encourage The Children: *"Sergio, what exercise is Teddy showing us today? Let's do it together." "Good for Vohny and Heather. You are exercising together."*

RAG DOLL: Relaxation exercises are also good for our bodies. Duplicate the relaxation strip and hang it at the children's eye level. When someone needs a break from play, go over and relax.

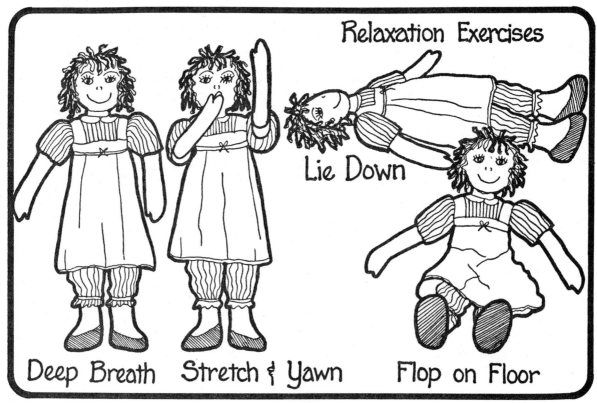

Relaxation Exercises

Lie Down

Deep Breath   Stretch & Yawn   Flop on Floor

168

Bend and Stretch Chart

Arm Circles & Swings

Jumping Jacks

Sit and Scoot

Lie Down & Kick

Touch the Floor

Hoops

HOOPLA: Duplicate the 'Warm-Up Chart' and glue it to a piece of colored construction paper. Hang it at the children's eye level in the large motor area. Have a child take a hoop and 'warm-up' by following the child in the chart and then moving his hoop around as he chooses.

Encourage The Children: Play 'Simon Says' with the hoops. You be Simon and give children directions on where to move the hoops. Switch places and let a child be Simon.

> Simon says, *"Hold the hoop in back/front of you."*
> Simon says, *"Try to touch the ceiling with your hoop."*
> Simon says, *"Put your head through the hoop."*
> Simon says, *"Put your hoop in your other hand and wave it."*
> Continue, ending with the last one.
> Simon says, *"Put your hoop on the floor and sit inside of it."*

COPY CAT: Have two or more children each take a hoop. One child begins moving his hoop and the other players copy him. Another player moves his hoop in a different way. The others copy him. Continue playing 'Copy Cat' with lots of different hoop movements.

EXERCISE HOOPS: Lay several hoops on the floor all very near or touching each other. Let the children move in and around each of the hoops as he chooses.
Encourage The Children: "Jan and Bob, you are dancing in the hoops. It looks like you're both moving your whole body." Count with the children as they exercise in a hoop. For example, as a child is jumping up and down, count "1, 2, 3, 4, 5, etc." Clap for him when he rests.

Warm-Up With Hoops

Mats

TUMBLE FREELY: Lay the tumbling mat in an open area. Let the children do tricks, exercises, and movements on it. Watch them for safety. *Encourage The Children: "Damon, how does your head feel when you're upside down?" "Matt, that was an interesting move. You rolled over and over and over, and then you jumped up at the other end of the mat."*

YOUR TURN: Have children sit or stand at one end of the mat. Say a child's name. He goes to the starting edge of the mat and announces to everyone what 'trick' he's going to do. He does it while everyone watches. When he's finished, he gets off of the mat while everyone claps for him. Name another child and continue playing.

SIMON SAYS: Have children sit or stand at one end of the mat. Call out a child's name. He goes to the starting edge of the mat. You say, "Simon says, 'Lauran, do a somersault.'" She does, and everyone claps. Continue having Simon give more directions.

ROLL DOWN THE MAT: Teach the children this song. Change it according to each child's name and the activity on the mat. (tumble, hop, swirl, somersault, cartwheel, etc.)

ROLL DOWN THE MAT
(Tune: Row, Row, Row, Your Boat)

Liz, Liz, Liz, Liz, (Child's name)
Roll down the mat.
Liz, Liz, Liz, Liz.
Roll back again.

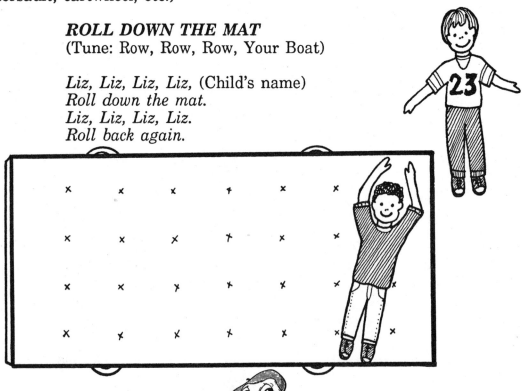

Movement and Records

GET THE BEAT: Let children choose favorite records or tapes and move freely to the rhythm.
Encourage The Children: "Andrea, you must really like the music you're listening to. You should see your smile. Let me take your picture." Clap the beat as children dance.

STREAMER DANCING: Get a dozen or more rubber rings such as for canning. Tie strips of plastic or fabric, scarves, streamers, or crepe paper to each one. Hang them on a hook near the music. Let the children hold one or two and move them as they dance.
Encourage The Children: "Brittany, you're waving your streamer way over your head." Give children directions as they are dancing, such as: "Sharice, wave your scarf behind you. That's it!" "Melody, can you make your streamer go in circles as you dance?"

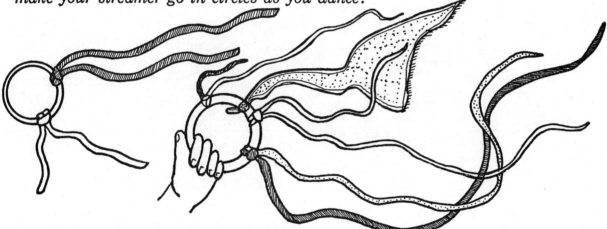

IN THE CENTER RING: Put one or more hoops on the floor. Let children dance to their favorite music inside the hoop.

PICK A PARTNER: Put several hoops near the music. Have two or more children hold one hoop, put on favorite music, and dance while holding the hoop.

SEE ME: Put a full length mirror near the music. Have the children dance in front of it and watch themselves and friends move.
Encourage The Children: "Watch your legs go!" "Patricia, you're waving your arms way above your head." "Can you see yourself in the mirror, Lamar?"

Ropes

WALK THE ROPE: Lay a 5' to 8' piece of clothesline on the floor. Have the children take off their shoes and walk from one end to the other. They could start by walking sideways along the rope and then when they feel more comfortable go heel to toe.

BALANCE ON A ROPE: Lay a piece of clothesline on the floor. Have one child stand on the rope and balance in that one spot. You or another child count as he balances. When you count to 5, have the child step off the rope and rest. As children gain confidence and skill, count to 7 or 10.
Encourage The Children: Let children pick the number you should count to. Thus, if a child says "3" or "8" then count to that number and then let the child rest.

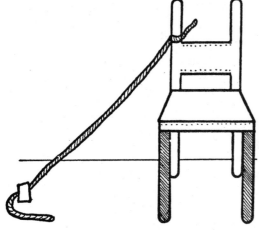

RAISE IT: Get an 8' to 10' clothesline. Tie one end of the rope to a chair and set it in an open space. Tape the other end of the rope to the floor.

Have the children step or jump over the rope wherever they choose. Maybe they would like to crawl or roll under it. After several days change the activity by taping the rope to a different spot on the floor. Another time tie the ropes between two chairs.
Encourage The Children: "Jimmy, you are playing 'Follow the Leader' with Dawn."
Ask a child, "Is it hard to jump over the rope?" Point to spots on the rope and let children choose whether they want to go over or under the rope in that place.

ROPE MAZES: Lay one clothesline on the floor with a lot of slack. Tape each end. Arrange the rope in an easy, squiggly configuration. Have children tiptoe, shuffle, walk, crawl, and move along it. Change the maze regularly. You could let children move the rope to create their own mazes.
EXTENSION: Tape two ropes parallel to each other. Move the ropes to create paths which children can move down, around, and over.

ROPING AROUND: Hang several short ropes from a hook. Let children create their own activities. They may want to work alone or in pairs.
Encourage The Children: "Karla, you and John are using all of your arm muscles in your tug-of-war." Have a child make a circle with a rope and then move in and out of it.

Swatters

MAKE SWATTERS: You'll need hangers, old nylon stockings, twist-ems, and heavy-duty tape. To make a swatter, pull out the triangle part of each hanger into a diamond shape. Stretch a nylon over the diamond shape and fasten it to the hanger with a twist-em or rubber band. Wrap tape around the hook of the hanger so that it is safe to hold.

GOLF: Get 5-8 spongeballs and a medium size box. Cut off the top of the box. Lay it on its side. Have the children put balls on the floor and gently tap them with their swatters across the floor into the box.

GOING HOME: Get 10-12 ping-pong balls. Using markers, draw faces on each one. Shape a medium size box into a house. Cut doors on several sides of the house. Using tape, make paths leading to each door. Have a child start at the beginning of a path and slowly tap a ping pong ball up the path and through the door. Help another 'smiley face' go home.

ROLL IT AROUND: Put a container of ping-pong balls or yarn balls near the swatters. Have a child put a ping-pong ball on his swatter. Holding the swatter with two hands, encourage him to roll the ball back and forth and around. If the ball rolls off, pick it up, and start again.

BALLOON TOSS: Blow up several small balloons and put them near the swatters. Let children gently bounce the balloons into the air with their swatters.

SWATTER HOCKEY: Mark-off a large area of your floor with a clothesline. Let two or more children each have a swatter. One child should gently 'swat' a sponge ball to another player. He 'swats' it back to the first player back or to a third child. Keep 'swatting' the ball, trying to keep it in the marked-off area. If the ball goes out of the area, simply get it and begin again.

175

Tape

TRIP ON A STRIP: Duplicate each picture of 'Maxi Mouse' doing her different movements. Cut each one out, back it with a piece of colored construction paper, and glue it to a paint stir stick. Stand each one in a thick piece of styrofoam.

   Put a long piece of wide colored tape on your floor. Place a picture of Maxi Mouse at one end of the tape. Have children look at the picture and decide how she is moving. The children should move along the strip that way. Change Maxi every couple of days.

Encourage The Children: *Maybe two children can take a 'trip on the strip' together.*

BACKWARDS

HOP ON TWO FEET

TIP-TOE

WALK

SKATE

CRAWL

Outside

MAKING TRACKS: Using chalk, mark off three separate tracks for children who want to walk, simply ride their vehicles, and race vehicles. Make signs and put them at the beginning of each track, so that children know what each track is for.

Encourage The Children: "Patrice, you're going to race your big wheel today. Did you remember to gas up? Let me check your tank. Looks full to me. Have a safe race." Suggest to the children on the walking track that they hop, skip, run, twirl, or move a way they think of.

BEANBAG TAG: Give the first player who is 'it' a beanbag. Say "Go" and the game begins. The player who is 'it' must tag another player with the beanbag. After being tagged, the player who was 'it' gives the beanbag to the player he tagged, and the game continues with a new 'it.'

OUTSIDE WALKS: Enjoy your neighborhood year-round by taking different types of walks. Just before you go back inside, run a couple of races.

- **Scarf Walk:** Before going on your walk, give everyone a scarf or streamer. As you're walking, look for birds. When you see one, wave to him with your scarf.

- **Shadow Walk:** Before going outside say this rhyme.

SHADOWS

Look to the left, look to the right.
Always keep your shadow in sight.
Liz Wilmes

Begin your walk. After awhile say, "Stop." The children stop and say the 'Shadows' rhyme as they look from side to side for their shadows. Ask the children to point to their shadows. Continue walking. Stop several more times, say the rhyme, and find shadows.

- **Quiet Walk:** Take a tablet of paper and a pencil with you on this walk. Ask the children to listen carefully for sounds in the neighborhood. When someone hears one he should wave his arms. Everyone stops and listens. Let a child name the sound. Write it down on the tablet. Continue walking. When you return to school read the list. On other 'quiet walks' add more sounds to your list.

- **Wiggly Walk:** As you're walking, look for creatures which wiggle and crawl along the sidewalk. Did you see worms? Caterpillars? Ants? Next time you take a 'wiggly walk' bring several magnifying glasses along so that you can look at the creatures even more closely.

- **Crack Walk:** As you're walking along the sidewalk, step on all of the cracks that you see. Another time pretend that the cracks are rivers.

- **Remember Walk:** Before going out, tell the children to remember all of the things that they see while walking. When you return to the room, get a large piece of paper and a marker. Have the children name what they saw. You make a list. Hang it on the door. Add to it as the children remember more things.

- **Vehicle Walk:** Stop along the sidewalk and look at all of the vehicles traveling along the road. Have the children name what they see. What was the largest/smallest one they saw.

- **Safety Walk:** As you're walking look for all of the safety signs. Talk about each one. When you get to a crossing, say this rhyme and then cross the intersection.

STOP, LOOK, LISTEN

We stop, we look, and we listen
Before we cross the street.
We use our eyes and ears
And then we use our feet.
Linda White and Sheri Shaefer

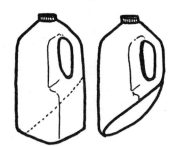

SCOOP IT: Collect 5-6 plastic milk bottles. Cut the bottoms out so that they become 'scoops.' Have a bucket of small balls available, (tennis, sponge, yarn). Let children play catch by tossing balls and catching them in their scoops.

IN THE SAND AREA: In warm weather have a source of water close-by, so that children always have a choice of using wet or dry sand. You can have a hose hooked up to a nearby faucet, spray bottles filled with water, or buckets of water with plastic pitchers or small scoops.

LADDER STUNTS: Lay one or more flat ladders on the ground. Let children walk rung to rung, space to space, heel to toe down one side of the ladder, etc. Turn the ladder on its side, hold the ends, and have fun going in and out of the openings. Have partners hold hands and do 'stunts' together.

ENJOY YOUR PLAY AREA: Use your outside space during all of the seasons.

- **Rake The Leaves:** Have small rakes and brooms. Let the children rake the leaves into large piles, jump into them, let the leaves fly, and rake them up again. As the weather gets colder, dispose of the leaves according to your community policies.

- **Shovel The Snow:** Have child-size shovels. Shovel snow into a huge pile. Climb, roll around, and dig in it. Use the snow to build a snowman. Lie in the snow to make snow creatures.

- **Plant A Garden:** In a small patch of dirt, plant flowers and/or vegetables. Care for your garden daily. Talk about what is happening.

- **Wash-Up:** On a nice warm day bring out buckets of water along with brushes and sponges. Wash all of the vehicles, equipment, and other outside materials.

... notes for myself ~

ADDITIONAL RESOURCES

- **Circle Time Book,** *Wilmes/Wilmes*. Active games, exercises, songs, and more for 39 holidays and seasons.
- **Everyday Circle Times,** *Wilmes/Wilmes*. Active games, exercises, songs, and more for 48 themes.
- **Games, Giggles, and Giant Steps,** *Miller*. Games for individuals and groups.
- **1,2,3 Games,** *Warren*. 70 no-loose group games.
- **Parachute Play,** *Wilmes/Wilmes*. Basic techniques plus 100 easy activities.
- **Yearful of Circle Times,** *Wilmes/Wilmes*. Active games, exercises, songs, and more for 52 different themes.

Manipulatives

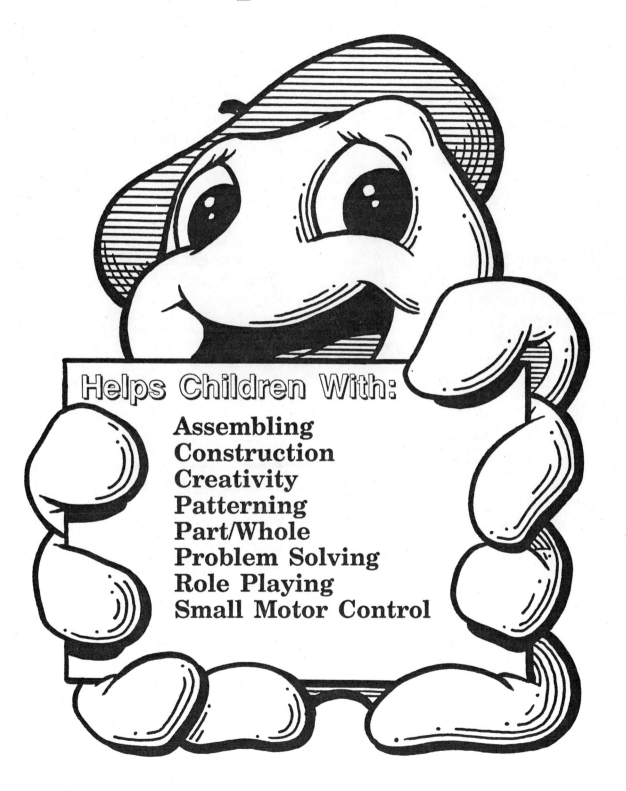

Helps Children With:

- Assembling
- Construction
- Creativity
- Patterning
- Part/Whole
- Problem Solving
- Role Playing
- Small Motor Control

Manipulatives
Supply List

Accessories

Airplanes
Automobiles
Beads
Blunt Plastic Needles
Boats
Bristle Blocks
Buttons
Checkers
Coffee Stir Sticks
Color Cubes
Colored Clothespins
Community Helpers
Disks
Dominoes
Duplo Blocks
Foam Blocks
Lacing Beads
Large Colored Clips
Legos
Lincoln Logs
Magnet Board
Magnetic Tape
Magnets
Masonite
Metal Paper Clips
Miniature Cars

Molded Styrofoam Packing
   Material (Television)
Parquetry Blocks
Pegboards
Pegs
People
Picture Cards
Poker Chips
Popsicle Sticks
Posterboard
Posters
Puzzles
Shoe Boxes
Shoe Laces
Small Wooden Blocks
Spools
Stickers
String
Tiles
Tongue Depressors
Trucks
Vehicles
Waffle Blocks
Wide Mouth Straws
Yarn

Clean-Up

Broom/Dustpan
Labeled Containers/Shelves
Sponges

184

SMALL BLOCK MIX AND MATCH: Offer a variety of small blocks with which the children can build as they choose.

- Label each of the block containers with a picture of the type of block stored in it. Put all of the different block containers close to each other on your manipulative shelf; thus, when children are deciding which blocks to use, the blocks are easily accessible.

- Have the different types of block accessories very visible and near the blocks.
  Encourage The Children: *"Nache, you have the nurse, doctor, fire fighter, and police officer on the floor. Are you going to use them with your building?" "Monica, you're stacking your blocks. How high are you trying to go?"*

INTRODUCING SMALL BLOCKS: Using colored tape, mark off a special area of a table or floor in which the children can build. Put a container of one type of block in the area. If children need more space, you can easily move the tape. Each time you set up this activity, offer the children a different set of blocks.
EXTENSION: As time goes on, offer more unusual 'blocks' such as checkers, dominoes, spools, tiles, playing cards, sponges, and so on.

MATCH IT: Get one type of block such as the color cubes. Sit next to a child. Set several blocks out in a specific order or pattern such as red-blue, red-blue, red-blue. Let the child you're sitting with build an identical block pattern next to yours. Once the child has built his blocks, touch each of yours and say the colors aloud. Let the child touch each of his and say the colors aloud. Do they match? If so, make another pattern; if not, talk about where the two patterns are the same and different.

Cards

CONCENTRATION: Cut 10-20, 2"x4" pieces of white posterboard. Get a set of stickers, such as colored smiley faces, which has multiples of each picture. Make pairs of smiley face cards, using all of the different colors.

To play, mix up all of the cards. Lay them face down on the table/floor. One player turns a card over and looks at it. Then he turns another card over and looks at it. If the cards match, the player takes them off of the grid; if not, he turns them back over. The next player turns a card over and looks at it. If they match, remove them; if not, turn them back over. Continue until all of the cards have been matched.

KATY-TWO-POCKETS: Using the pattern on page 187 as a guide, make a 'Katy-Two-Pockets' out of posterboard. Use her to play different card games.

- **Pairs:** Get a set of cards which have identical pairs. Put one card in Katy's top pocket. Find the mate and put it in her other pocket. Continue pairing.

- **Name It:** Get a set of cards with pictures on them. Have a child lay a card on the top pocket and name the object being pictured. Have him lay another card on the bottom pocket and name it. Continue until he's put all of the cards in Katy's pockets.

- **Go-Togethers:** Buy or make cards which have pictures of things which logically go together, such as a toothbrush/toothpaste, fire-fighter/fire truck, tree/leaf, and so on. Put a card in one of Katy's pockets. Find its mate and put it in the other pocket. Continue finding and putting the 'go-togethers' in Katy's pockets.

END-TO-END: Get a set of stickers, such as fruit, which has multiples of each picture. Cut 8-10, 2"x4" white posterboard rectangles. Divide each posterboard card in half with a marker. On the first card put the sticker of an apple and a banana; on the second card start with the banana and add a different fruit (pineapple) to the right side. On the third card have banana/pineapple. Continue this way, always repeating the previous fruit on the left side of each card and adding a new fruit to the right side.

To play, mix up all of the cards. Put one card on the table/floor. Name the two fruits. Find the card which has a matching fruit and lay it next to the first one. Continue until all of the cards have been laid end-to-end. VARIATION: "Andre, you've got the cards with fruit stickers on them. You know we're going to have fruit for a snack today. I think we've got bananas. Find a card with a picture of a banana."

Colorful Board Games

GO FISH: Using the patterns on page 189 as a guide, cut out a lake from blue posterboard and different colored fish from construction paper. Slip a metal paper clip onto each one. Make several fishing poles with short handles and strings. Tie magnets on the end of the strings.

Set the lake on the table and stock it with the fish. Let the children stand near the lake and fish. *Encourage The Children: "Bo, what color fish did you just catch?" "Samantha, you just caught a green fish didn't you? Try to get that purple one over there."*

GOOD NIGHT TEDDY: Using the illustration on page 190 as a guide, make a giant teddy bear wearing his polka dot pajamas. From posterboard cut out pairs of colored polka dots to fit on Teddy's pajamas.

Set Teddy on the table along with the container of polka dots. Let the children add pairs of colored polka dots to Teddy's pajamas.
VARIATION: Play this game with a friend. One child puts one polka dot on Teddy's pajamas, and the other player finds the matching polka dot and puts it on the pajamas.

PIZZA BOX GAMES: Go to your local pizza restaurant and buy several pizza boards and the boxes that they fit in, or cut pieces of white posterboard into large circles. Divide the boards into eight equal sections. Cut eight different pieces of colored construction paper the exact size of the sections on each board. Using spray or watered-down white glue, glue the colored sections to the boards. Cover them with clear adhesive paper.

- **Park It:** Get small cars the same colors as the wheel. Pretend that each section is a different garage. Drive all of the cars to their proper garages and park them. Store the board and cars in one of the pizza boxes. Label it. (See page 191.)

- **Make A Pie:** Using colored posterboard, cut pieces of pie to match each section of the wheel. Prepare your delicious pie by matching the colored pieces to the pie shell. Serve the pie to friends. "I would like a piece of chocolate pie." Store the pie and pieces in one of the pizza boxes. Label it. (See page 191.)

- **Clip It:** Get a bag of colored clothespins. Set it on the table along with the color wheel. Let the children clip the clothespins to the matching sections. Store the pie and pieces in one of the pizza boxes. Label it.

190

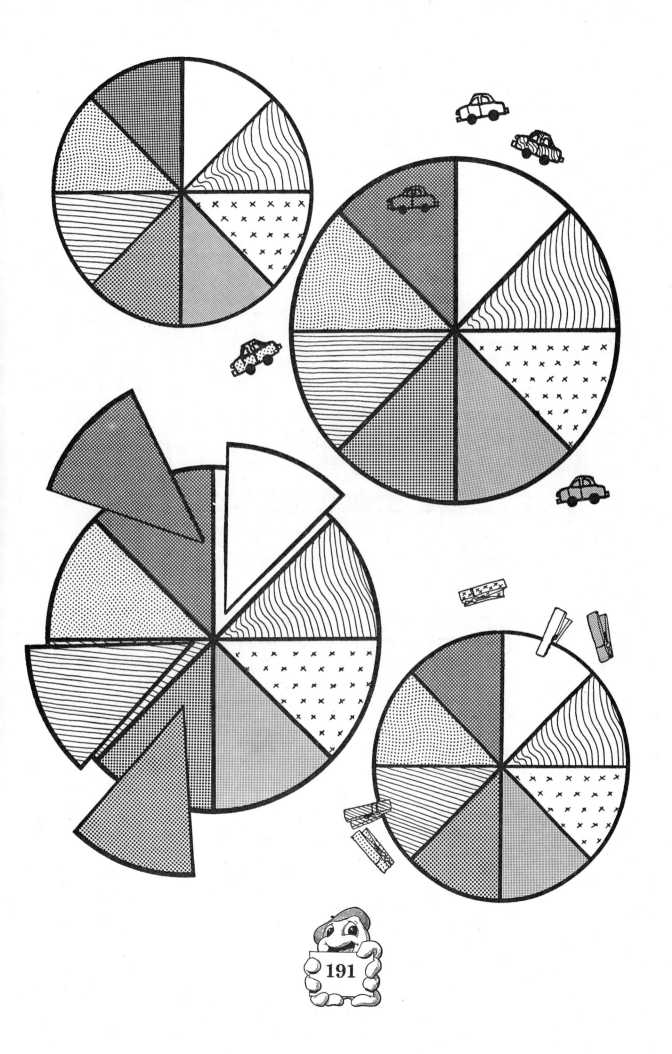

Dramatic Play

IMAGINATION YARN: Cut 3-4 pieces of heavy yarn, each several feet long. Tape one end of each piece to a table. (Not too close together.) Have children form the yarn into different designs, squiggles, and shapes.
EXTENSION: Get a small container and put a variety of people, vehicles, and animals in it. Have the children form the yarn into homes, zoos, tracks, and so on, and add the accessories as they pretend.

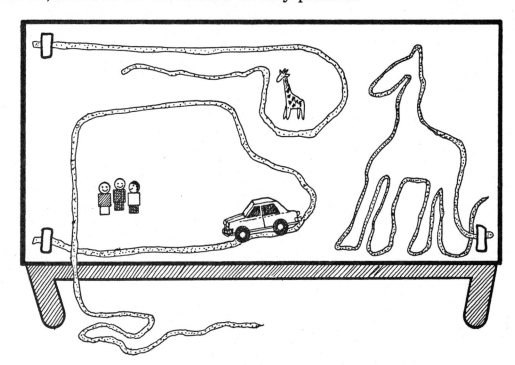

PLAY BOARDS: Get 3 large pieces of corrugated cardboard, posterboard, or large shallow bakery boxes that donuts and sweet rolls are delivered in. Using the designs of the town, farm, and airport on the next three pages as a guide, make different simple play boards. First draw in all of the roads, parking lots, tracks, and so on. Then use paint to color in the fields, lakes, and grassy areas.

Put a play board on the table/floor along with a container of accessories such as boats, airplanes, trucks, cars, people, animals, tires, etc.

Encourage The Children: "Clydale, you want the airport. Here it is. What else do you need? Here is the container. You can pick the pieces you'd like to use." "I see that you and your friends are at the airport, Carrington. Are you all going to take an airplane ride? Where are you going?"

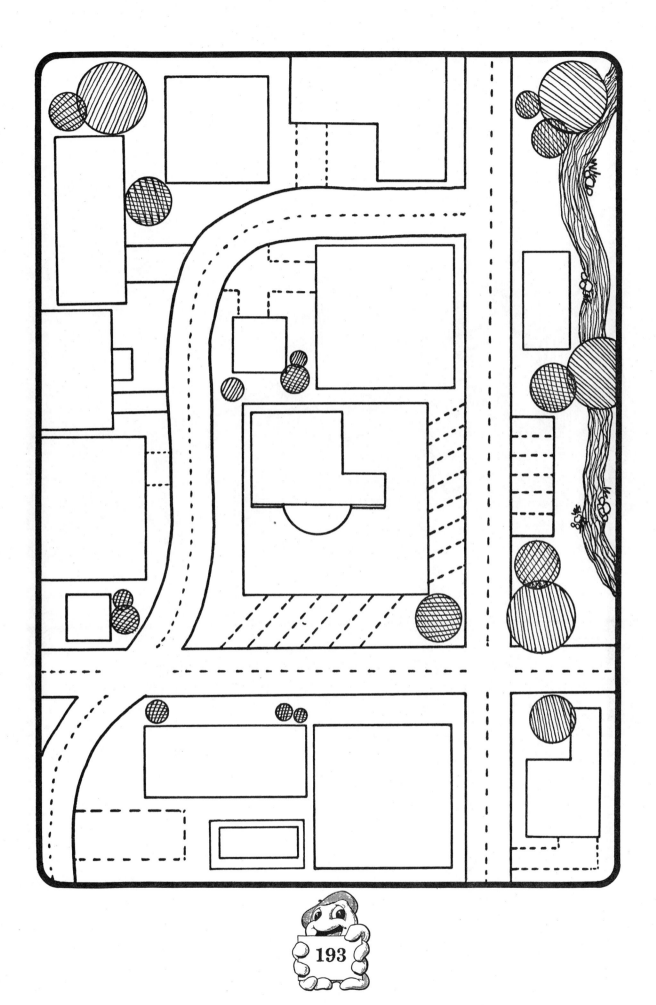

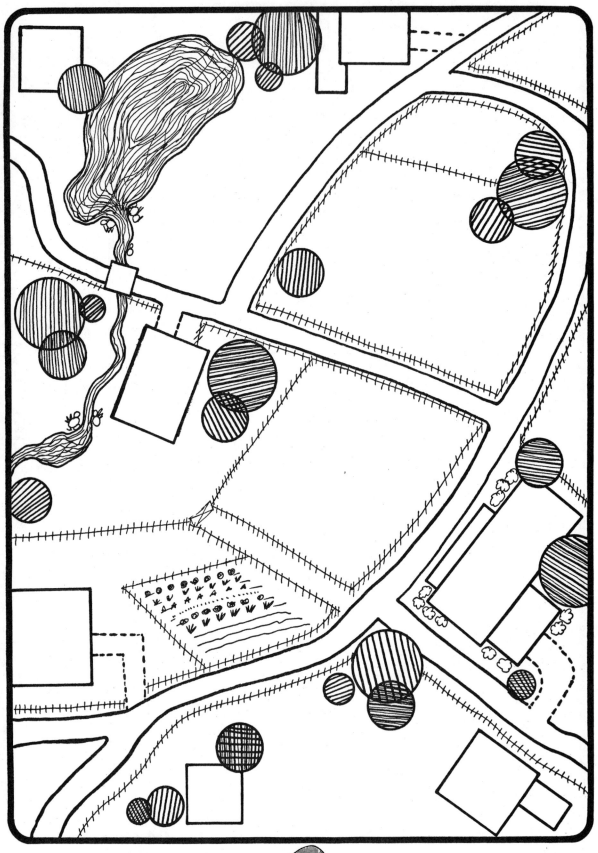

194

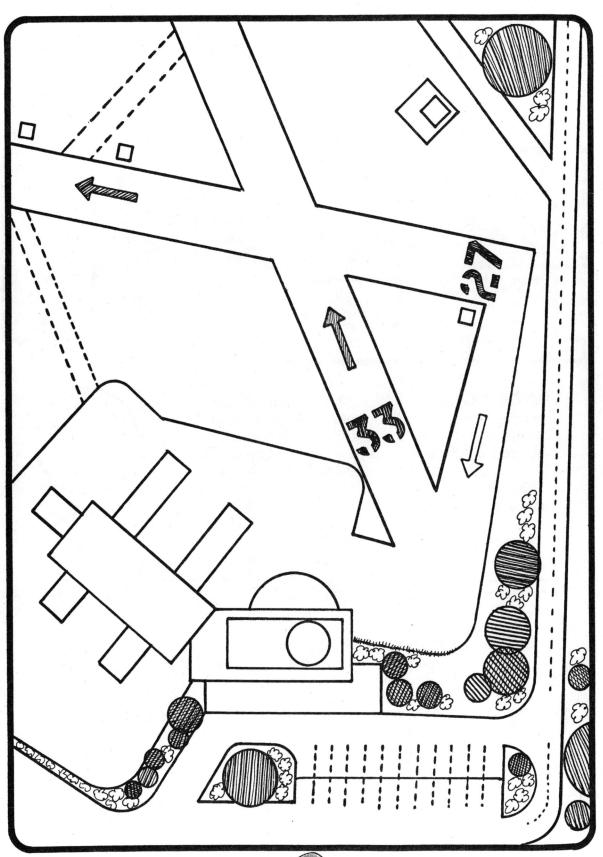

195

Magnet Board*

CREATE-A-DESIGN: Put magnetic shapes on a tray. (Make your own by cutting out twenty or more shapes from different colors of posterboard and gluing a piece of magnetic tape to the back of each one.) Put the pieces in a small basket next to the magnet board. Let the children move some or all of the pieces around creating different colorful designs.

YES OR NO: Make 1, 4" diameter smiling and frowning face out of posterboard. Cut out 15 to 20 pictures of different toys. Laminate or cover the faces and pictures with clear adhesive paper. Glue a piece of magnetic tape to the back of each one.

Put the faces at the top of the magnet board. Have a child look at a picture of one of the toys and decide if he would like to play with it or not. If he would, put it on the smiling side; if not, stick it to the frowning side. Continue with all of the pictures. VARIATION: Instead of using pictures of toys, use vehicles, foods, clothes, or animals.

BUILD A CONE: Use the pattern of the ice cream cone on the next page to make a posterboard cone and all of the scoops. Glue a piece of magnetic tape on the back of each piece. Put the pieces in a sturdy ice cream container.

Let a child build an ice cream cone by putting the cone at the bottom of the magnet board and adding the scoops from largest to smallest or vice versa.

* If you do not have a magnet board you can use an automobile oil pan from the automotive department.

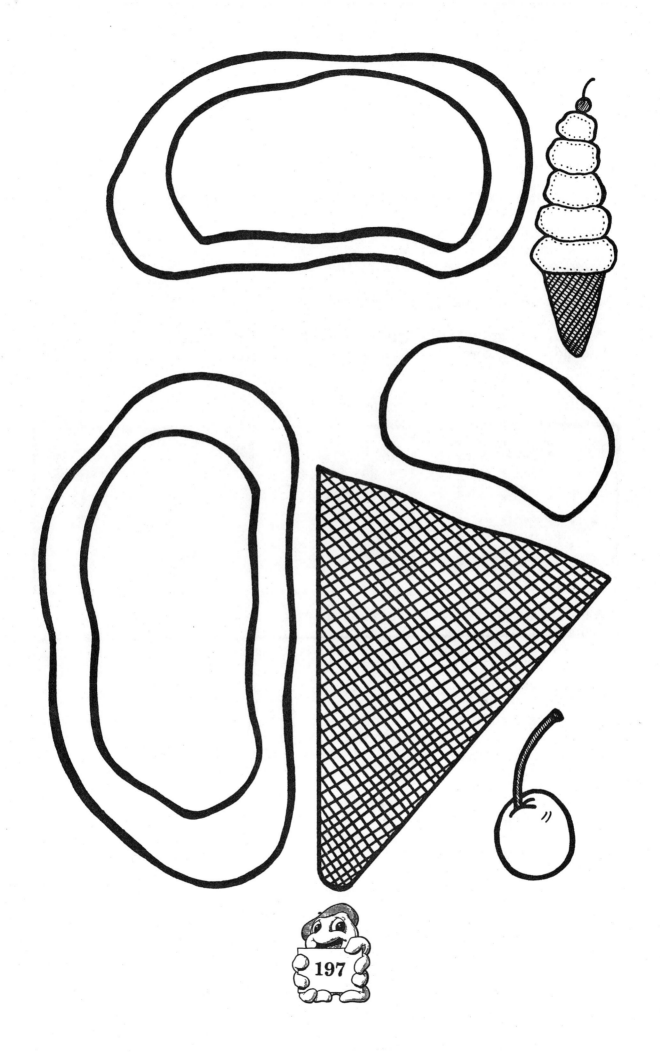

197

Pegboards

PEGBOARD PLAY: Set up a variety of activities to help the children use the pegboard in different ways.

- **Mix and Match:** Put the pegboard out with a container of pegs. Let the children make designs, poke pegs into holes, and talk about the colors of the pegs they are choosing.
Encourage The Children: "Victor, you're filling your pegboard with all red pegs. Are you going to keep that up or use different colors?" "Sharon, you're putting your pegs around the outside of your pegboard." "Greg, you've almost filled up your entire pegboard!"

- **Design Sheets:** Using markers, make simple design sheets which the children can copy. To make each sheet cut a piece of white posterboard the same size as your pegboard. Make black dots for each hole. Using colored markers to match the colors of your pegs, mark out simple designs. Laminate each one or cover it with clear adhesive paper.

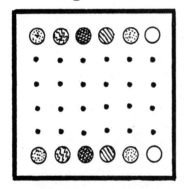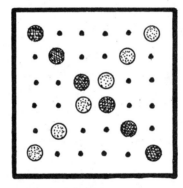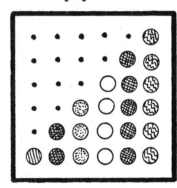

- **Numeral Strips:** Make numeral strips to use with the pegboard. To make each strip cut a piece of posterboard the same dimensions as one row of your pegboard. Make black dots for each hole. On the first strip write "1" on the first dot. On the second strip write "1,2" on the first two dots. Continue in this manner until you've made number strips for at least all of the holes in one row of the pegboard.

  Have a child pick the number strip he would like to peg and put it above one row on the pegboard. Now he should put that number of pegs on his board. Take the pegs out, choose a different strip, and peg some more.

● **Color Strips:** Using colored markers, make color strips for the pegboard. To make each strip, cut a piece of white posterboard the same dimensions as one row of your pegboard. Make black dots for each hole. Using a single color, mark over each dot.

Have a child pick the strip he would like to use and decide which row he is going to peg. Have him place his strip above the row he will use. Now he can begin matching his pegs to his color strip.
EXTENSION: Make color strips using various colors.

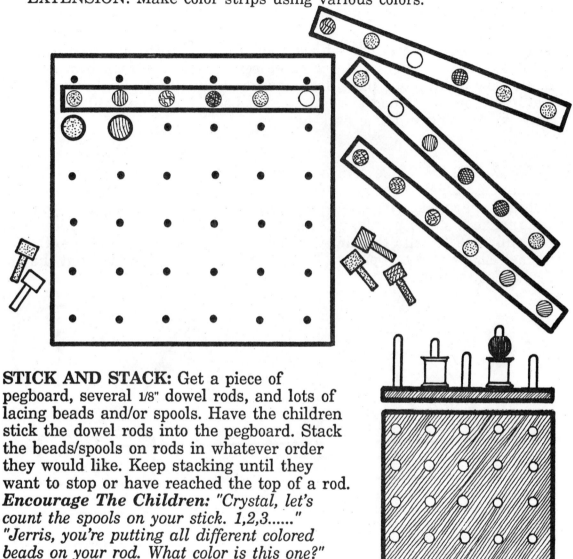

STICK AND STACK: Get a piece of pegboard, several 1/8" dowel rods, and lots of lacing beads and/or spools. Have the children stick the dowel rods into the pegboard. Stack the beads/spools on rods in whatever order they would like. Keep stacking until they want to stop or have reached the top of a rod. *Encourage The Children: "Crystal, let's count the spools on your stick. 1,2,3......" "Jerris, you're putting all different colored beads on your rod. What color is this one?"*

STICK IT: Get a large piece of molded styrofoam. Take a knife and cut lots of various length slits in it. Highlight the slits with magic marker by drawing a line along each one. Have a container of popsicle sticks. Let children stick them into the slits in whatever order they would like.
VARIATION: Instead of pushing popsicle sticks into the styrofoam, try a container of large colored paper clips, poker chips, tongue depressors, or coffee stir sticks.

199

Puzzles

PUZZLE PLAY: Sit with the children as they do puzzles.

- **Switch:** As the children are playing with puzzles, you do one also. When you have finished yours, ask a child if he'd like to switch puzzles with you. Do your new puzzle. Switch again.

- **Turn It Over:** Do a puzzle with a child. Start with it completed. Have him take each piece out of the puzzle, look at it, and turn it over on the table. Now pick up one piece, look at it, and put it back in the puzzle tray. Turn over a second piece and put it back. Continue until you and he have put the entire puzzle back together.

DESIGN PUZZLES: Make your own simple puzzle boards with accompanying miniature puzzles. To make each puzzle board, cut a large posterboard shape featuring the theme of the puzzle. For example, if you are going to make a shape puzzle, cut out a large triangle. Cut 5-6 smaller shapes which all fit onto the large triangle. Trace around each shape. Cut each small shape into two pieces. To play, mix up the pieces and put the small puzzles together.

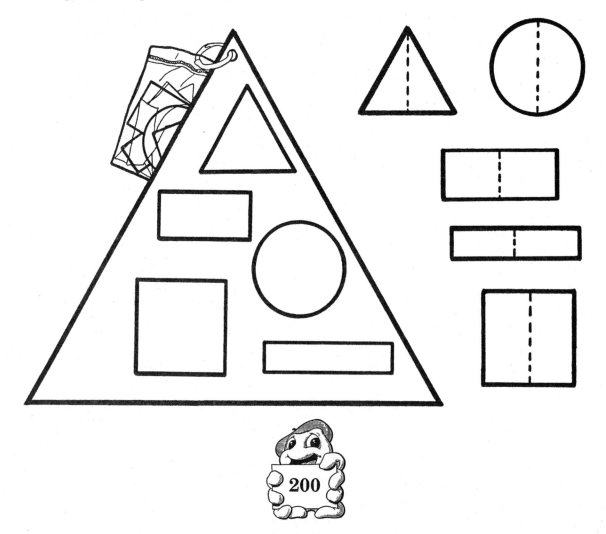

VARIATION: In addition to the shape puzzle, make a giant snowball board/regular size snowballs, a dinosaur board/smaller dinosaurs, a pumpkin board/jack-o-lanterns, or a giant jelly bean board/colored jelly beans.

FLOOR PUZZLES: On full size pieces of posterboard, draw simple figures such as a gingerbread character, a snowman, a heart, a kite, and so on. Cut out the figures. Add as much detail to each one as you want. Cut up each figure into as many pieces as would be appropriate for the children. Store the pieces in an envelope. Draw a picture of the puzzle on the front of each envelope.

POSTER PUZZLES: Collect posters appropriate for your children. Glue them onto posterboard. Laminate or cover them with clear adhesive paper. Cut up each poster into as many pieces as would be appropriate for your children. Store them in clear resealable bags, so that you can easily see which poster puzzle is in each bag.

Stringing

STRINGING MIX AND MATCH: Offer the children a variety of materials to string. Remember to tie the first object onto the string to avoid the frustration of it slipping off.

- Large beads on a piece of rope.

- Small beads, disks, and buttons on shoe laces.

- Spools on pieces of heavy yarn. Thread blunt-tipped needles with yarn. Tie a large knot or a bead near the end of the yarn. Use the needles to string the spools.

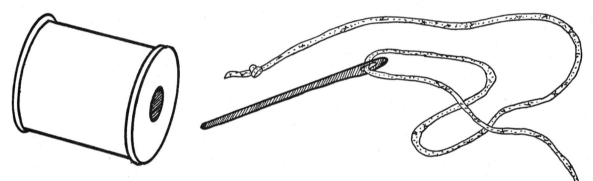

STRING A NECKLACE: Give children opportunities to string different necklaces, arm bands, crowns, bracelets, and belts.

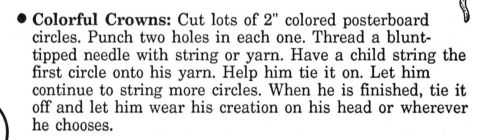

- **Colorful Crowns:** Cut lots of 2" colored posterboard circles. Punch two holes in each one. Thread a blunt-tipped needle with string or yarn. Have a child string the first circle onto his yarn. Help him tie it on. Let him continue to string more circles. When he is finished, tie it off and let him wear his creation on his head or wherever he chooses.

- **Noodle Necklaces:** Have children watercolor lots of mostaciolli and rigatoni noodles. After they are dry, let the children string the noodles onto colorful yarn. As children finish, help them tie off the ends and decide where they are going to wear their jewelry.

- **Buttons and Straws:** Cut wide-mouth straws into various lengths. Have a container of buttons. Help children thread blunt-tipped needles with heavy-duty thread. Remember to tie on the first piece at the end of the thread. Let children string all types of jewelry to wear.

Lacing

LACING MIX AND MATCH: Offer the children a variety of materials to lace.

- Have the dressing frames available which accent lacing and tying.

- Put the lacing pegs and laces out with your pegboard. Let children randomly put the pegs in the board and then lace them together.

LACE-UP: Glue a pair of shoes which can be laced to a piece of posterboard or thin plywood. Tie a lace to the first eyelet on each shoe. Let the children practice lacing and unlacing the shoes.
Encourage The Children: *"Monica, you're wearing shoes with laces. Did you lace them yourself?" "Kyle, let me help you lace the shoe. That's right, stick the lace through this eyelet and pull it up. Take the other end and stick the lace through this eyelet and pull up. Good start! Keep going."*

WORM IN AN APPLE: Cut several large apples from posterboard. Punch 4 or 5 holes in a squiggly line (like a worm) in each one. Cut pieces of heavy brown yarn. Wrap a piece of tape around one end of the yarn to make a needle. Let children weave the worms through the apples.
EXTENSION: Cut other simple shapes out of colored posterboard. Punch holes around the edges of each shape. Tape a long shoe lace to the back of each lacing card.

Teach the children this rhyme to chant as they use the lacing cards.

UP-DOWN

Up, down; up, down.
Up, down and all around.

Outside

BUCKET OF FUN: Gather 25-50 of the same object such as crayons, small blocks, poker chips, or clothespins. Put the sets of objects in buckets. Cut posterboard into 11"x14" cards. Lay one object, such as a clothespin, in the upper left-hand corner of one card. Trace around it. Continue tracing the object until the card is full. Pick different objects and make more cards.

Bring one card and a bucket of the matching objects outside. Put them on a table and let the children match the objects to the pictures. Another day bring out a different card and bucket of matching objects. ***Encourage The Children:*** *"Nel, you are laying all of the clothespins on the board. What color are you putting down now?"*

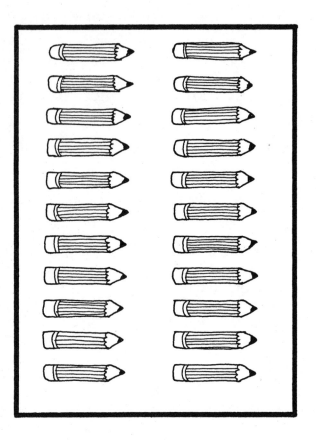

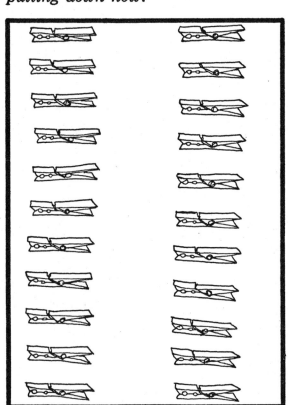

... *notes for myself* ~

ADDITIONAL RESOURCES

- **Do Touch,** *Gilbert*. Create activities using sponges, stickers, cups, and more.
- **Felt Board Fun,** *Wilmes/Wilmes*. Activities plus patterns.
- **I Can Do It! I Can Do It!** *Gilbert*. Activities for sorting, matching, pairing, mixing, etc.
- **Make-Take Games,** *Wilmes/Wilmes*. Instructions and illustrations to make 32 games.
- **Make-Take Games Companion Pattern Set.** 21 giant pattern sheets to make the 32 games. Patterns easily adapted to make other games.
- **Mathematics Their Way,** *Baratta-Lorton*. Activities for patterning, measuring, comparing, counting, recognizing numbers, etc.
- **Pocketful of Miracles Set 1,** *Eisenhart*. File folder games to make for year around.
- **Pocketful of Miracles Set 2,** *Eisenhart*. File folder games to make for holidays.
- **Workjobs Set 1,** *Baratta-Lorton*. Use everyday materials to make math and language games.
- **Workjobs Set 2,** *Baratta-Lorton*. Use everyday materials to make language games.

Sand/Water

Helps Children With:

Construction
Creativity
Measuring
Motor Control
Quantity
Relaxation
Self Confidence
Tactile Stimulation

Sand/Water

Supply List

Sand Clean-Up

Child-Size Brooms
Dust Pans
Put sand accessories in a
   large mesh bag and
   rinse off. Hang the bag
   up to dry overnight.

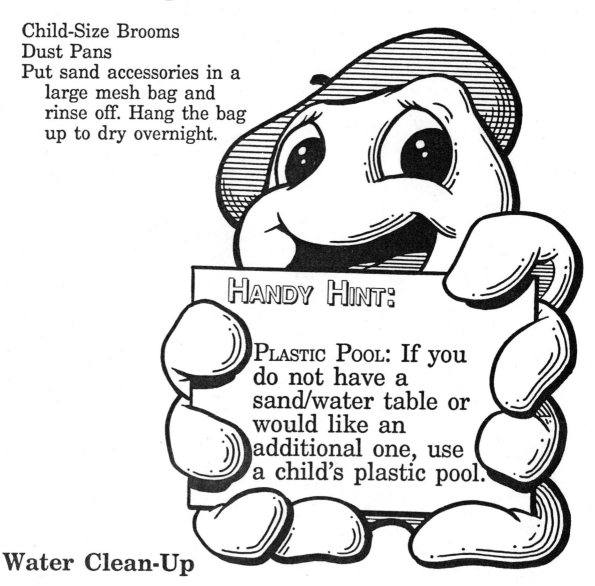

HANDY HINT:

PLASTIC POOL: If you do not have a sand/water table or would like an additional one, use a child's plastic pool.

Water Clean-Up

Bucket
Dish Rack
Mop
Sponges
Towels

Accessories

Animals
Balance Scale
Basters
Birthday Candles
Boats
Bottle Caps
Bubble Wrap
Buttons
Cardboard Tubes
Cars
Checkers
Clothespins
Coffee Scoops
Coffee Stir Sticks
Colanders
Colored Acetate
Combs
Cookie Cutters
Corks
Dish Tubs
Dolls
Dowel Rods
Egg Beaters
Egg Cartons
Film Canisters
Fingernail Brushes
Food Coloring
Forks
Funnels
Ketchup Containers
Knives (Dull)
Liquid Detergent
Magnifying Glasses
Margarine Tubs
Measuring Cups
Measuring Scoops
Measuring Spoons
Molds

Molded Styrofoam
    Packing Material
    (i.e. around
    television sets)
Muffin Tins
Pails
Paint Stir Sticks
People
Pie Tins
Pitchers
Plastic Pizza Cutters
Plastic Straws
Poker Chips
Popsicle Sticks
Rakes
Rocks
Salt/Other Shakers
Sand
Shells
Sieves
Sifters
Slated Spoons
Spatulas
Sponges
Spoons
Spray Bottles
Stones
Straws
Styrofoam Trays
Toilet Paper Tubes
Tongs
Tongue Depressors
Towels
Trucks
Washers (metal)
Wash Tubs
Watering Cans
Whisks

Sand

EXPLORING SAND: Give the child many opportunities to use the sand without any accessories.

- Build hills, sift sand through your fingers, push it around with your hands, dig holes, and so on.
  Encourage The Children: Play with them. "Dick, let's push all of the sand to the middle and see if we can build a mountain." "Liz, let's wiggle our fingers in the sand. How does it feel?"

- Put a spray bottle filled with a little water near the sand. Let the children wet down the sand and play. They can make prints, dig tunnels, mold shapes, and so on.

- Have several small trays and magnifying glasses. Put a little sand on a tray and look at it very carefully with the magnifying glass.
  Encourage The Children: "What do you see?" "What colors are in the sand?" "Do you see any larger/smaller pieces of sand?"

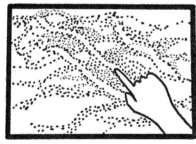

- Fill a spray bottle with a little water, wet down the sand, and play 'Copy Cat' with the children. Using your finger/s, draw a very simple design in the sand. Have a child or children copy your design. Erase the designs; let someone make another one and the other players copy it. Play this often when you have a minute or more.

- Periodically put a different type of sand in the sand table for the children to explore and play in. For example, try a new texture of sand such as very coarse or very fine. Try a different color of sand such as white, black, or a various shade of brownish-yellow.

SCOOP-POUR-DUMP: Mix and match a few accessories at a time so that children can dig, pour back and forth, scoop and shift, fill and empty containers, and so on.

- Have an assortment of different size containers. *Encourage The Children:* *"Sheila, you're using the smallest container for a scoop. Are you going to fill all of the other tubs?" "Jake, you're using your hand for a shovel. How does it work?"*

- Have 5-6 coffee scoops with 2-3 large containers. *Encourage The Children:* *"Jo, you and Jeremy are both trying to fill that big pail. Keep scooping!" "Jack, I hear you counting. Can I count with you?"*

- Have several pie pans plus an assortment of different spoons ranging in size from small plastic ones to large slatted ones.

- Offer 3 or 4 pairs of pitchers, each pair being a different size.

SAND MIX AND MATCH: Offer the children different accessories to encourage them to pretend.

- Have a variety of small vehicles and a spray bottle filled with water.

- Have some cookie cutters, molds, spoons, and birthday candles. *Encourage The Children:* *"Whose birthday is it, Malcomb? Let's sing 'Happy Birthday' together."*

- Put a large packing mold in the middle of the sand. Add zoo animals, popsicle sticks, tongue depressors, and miniature people. *Encourage The Children:* *"Tell me what you're doing here, Sarah." "Marguirita, do you go to the zoo? What animals do you see there?"*

POKE-A-FIGURE: Put the 'Poke-A-Figure Stencils' and several spray bottles filled with a little water on a table near the sand. Children can choose stencils, smooth out the sand, wet it down a little, and poke the stencils with their fingers, popsicle sticks, or other accessories. When they lift their stencils up -- presto -- they've poked a figure. Erase it and poke another one. ***Encourage The Children:*** *"Carol, what stencil did you choose?" "Hey, Jamie, you really poked deep holes. Let's see the finger you used." "Marcella, what did you poke? Yes, it looks like a square. Are you going to poke a circle and a triangle too? Show me when you're done."*

POKE-A-FIGURE STENCILS

<u>You'll Need:</u>
Large Styrofoam Trays
Pencil

<u>To Make:</u> Draw a simple outline of a design, shape, or object on a tray. Using a pencil, poke holes about 1" to 1½" apart around the outline. Make each hole larger by poking it with your index finger.

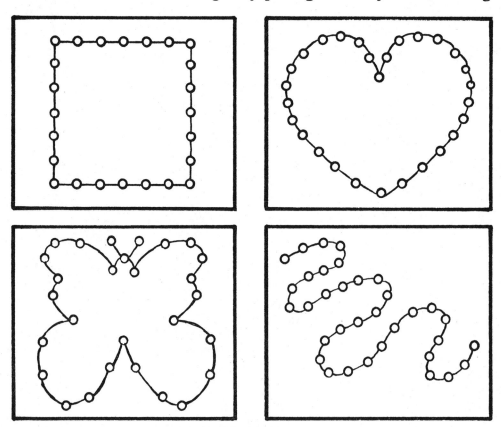

DRAW-A-DESIGN: Put a basket filled with unsharpened pencils, popsicle sticks, tongue depressors, heavy-duty toothpicks, paint stir sticks, and sand combs along with several spray bottles filled with water near the sand. ***Encourage The Children:*** *"Adele, you're drawing your design with your fingers. Are you having fun? Do you want to tell me about your drawing?" "Chester, your design has deep holes in it. How did you make those?"*

SAND COMBS

<u>You'll Need</u>:
    Giant Plastic Combs
    Scissors

<u>To Make</u>: Cut teeth out of the combs to make different designs. Use these combs to make a variety of squiggles through the sand.

CARDBOARD SAND COMBS

<u>You'll Need</u>:
    Heavy-Duty Cardboard
    Scissors or Mat Knife

<u>To Make</u>: Cut the cardboard into 3"x8" rectangles. Draw a different comb design along the bottom edge of each rectangle. Cut out the design. Use the cardboard combs to make lots of designs.

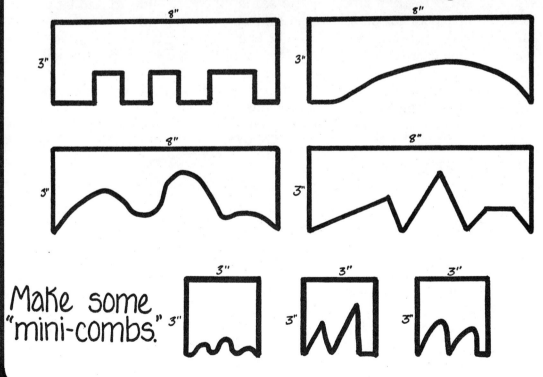

Make some "mini-combs."

HIDE 'N SEEK: Hide objects in the sand and let the children find them.

- **Sand Concentration:** Hide pairs of small objects in the sand. (shells, poker chips, giant paper clips, erasers, small blocks, small cars, stones, straws, etc.) Have the children feel around in the sand with both of their hands. When a child thinks he's found a pair, pull out the objects and see. Were they a pair? Hide them again and search for another pair. VARIATION: Have a tray near the sand table. As children find pairs, have them set the objects next to each other on the tray. After the children have found all of the pairs, put them back in the sand and hunt again.

- **Sand Shake:** Pour several inches of sand into a 2 liter plastic bottle and then fill it about 2/3 full with water. Have children shake it up and watch -- shake and watch -- shake and watch.

  Once the children are familiar with how the sand and water look when they are settled and mixed, secretly add an object to it, like a stone, small shell, bead, coin, or piece of rope. Now let the children shake the bottle and find the object. What is it? Where is it? Shake again. Now where is it?

- **Keep Looking:** Gather 20-60 of the same object to hide in the sand. (rubber bands, pencils, plastic forks and spoons, inch blocks, milk bottle caps, etc.) Make a large 'Hide 'N Seek Card' for each set of objects. Hide one set of objects in the sand. Lay the matching 'Hide 'N Seek Card' on a table near the sand. Have children search for the objects. When a child finds one he should lay it on the 'Hide 'N Seek Card.' Continue until all of the objects are found. Hide the objects and play again.

HIDE 'N SEEK CARDS

<u>You'll Need:</u>
  Posterboard
  Objects you're going to hide

<u>To Make:</u> Cut the posterboard into 11"x14" pieces. Lay an object from the set in the upper left-hand corner of one of the pieces. Trace around it. Leaving space between each one, make as many images of the object as possible.

FOR A CHANGE: Take the sand out of your table and put something else in for several days: pieces of colored yarn, pieces of colored telephone wire, clothespins, checkers, bottle caps, buttons, or bubble wrap. Let the children explore and use the new materials as they wish. If the children need scoops, pails, or other accessories, have them available.

BALANCING ACT: Put the balance scale, the scoops, and different size small containers in the sand. Let the children experiment with the variety of containers and amounts of sand.
Encourage The Children: *"You almost have the two sides balanced, Malone. Which container are you going to put more sand in? I'll watch you."* *"Oh, Mary, you have two small containers on one side and a larger container on the other. Those should be fun to balance. Which container are you going to add sand to first?"*

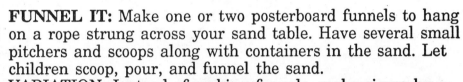

FUNNEL IT: Make one or two posterboard funnels to hang on a rope strung across your sand table. Have several small pitchers and scoops along with containers in the sand. Let children scoop, pour, and funnel the sand.
VARIATION: Instead of making funnels, make sieves by poking holes in the cone. Now when children scoop and pour the sand, watch what happens.

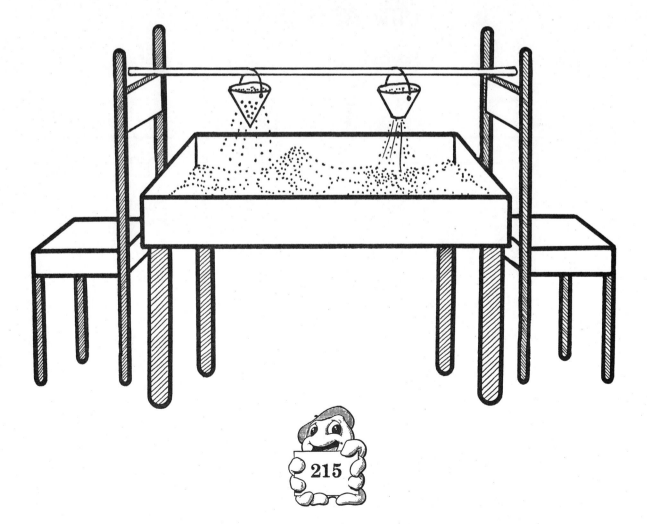

SCOOP IT UP: Make different sand toys from clean bleach bottles.

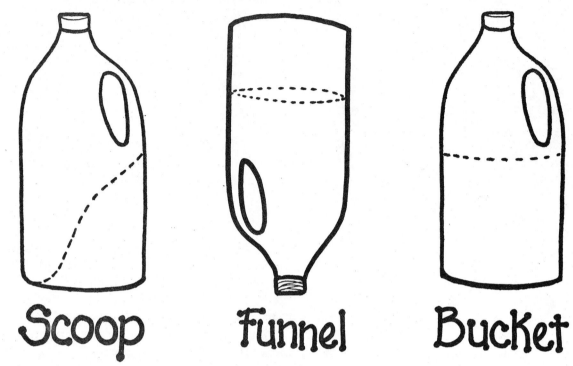

Scoop   Funnel   Bucket

Cut bottle as shown above.

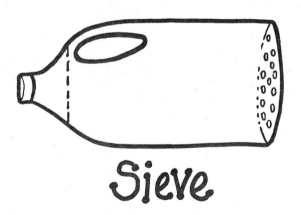

Sieve

Punch holes in the bottom of the bottle. Cut off top.

FOOTPRINTS IN THE SAND: With water from spray bottles or a trickle from a nearby hose, wet down the sand in your large sand area. Let the children take off their shoes and slowly walk through the sand making footprints.

Encourage The Children: Have the children look at their footprints. Can they find their toes? Heels? Look carefully for the arches.

Water

EXPLORING WATER: Give children many opportunities to use water without any accessories.
Encourage The Children: *Play with them. Use your hands to make small waves, scoop water into your hands and watch it drain through your fingers, swirl it with your fingers, blow it around, and so on.*

- Let the children help you add food coloring to the water. What color is the water today?

- Fill your water table with a different temperature of water than you normally do -- a little colder or a little warmer.
  VARIATION: Make lots of ice cubes ahead of time. Fill your water table about a third to half full of water. Let the children use it for awhile. Then bring out the ice cubes. Pour them into the water. Continue playing.
  Encourage The Children: *"How does the water feel now, Carlos?" "Jimmy, would you like to take a bath in this temperature of water? Why? Why not?"*

- Put rocks on the bottom of the water table. Make a simple periscope. Gently slide it into the water. Let the water calm down and look at the rocks. Very slowly move the periscope and look at different rocks.

SIMPLE PERISCOPE

You'll Need:
   Coated Cardboard
      Milk Container
   Clear Plastic Wrap
   Rubber Bands
   Tape

<u>To Make:</u> Cut off the top and bottom of the milk carton. Put a long piece of plastic wrap on the table. Set the milk carton in the middle of the wrap. Bring the wrap up the sides of the carton and into the top. Tape the wrap inside the top of the carton. Slip several rubber bands up the carton to help hold the plastic wrap tightly to the sides.

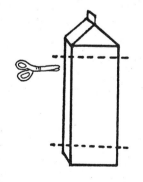 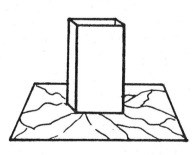  

FILL AND POUR: Mix and match a few accessories at a time so that children can make waves, pour back and forth, fill and empty containers, and so on.

- Have muffin tins and a set of measuring scoops.
  Encourage The Children: *"Maggie, you're using the smallest scoop to fill that muffin cup. Are you going to fill all of the cups in the pan? I'll be back to see how it's going?"*

- Have several watering cans along with pails and small margarine tubs.
  Encourage The Children: *"Jack, you've filled all of the margarine tubs. What next?" "Willie, you're watering the water in the table. Oh I see, it's your garden. Tell me what you're growing."*

- Have several sets of graduated size plastic containers such as the set of peanut butter or mayonnaise containers.

- Get a giant pail. Put it in the center of the water table. Set a brick or rock in it so that it does not float. Add several small pitchers. Using the pitchers, fill the giant pail with water. This could easily take several days.

WATER MIX AND MATCH: Offer children different accessories to encourage them to pretend.

Cut a styrofoam egg carton into different sized pieces. Have these and a container of miniature people near the water.

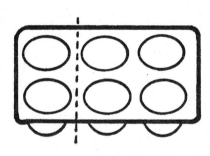  

- Have different sized rocks and stones and small sponges available.
  Encourage The Children: *"Jonah, you and Greg look like you're washing all of the rocks. I see you have a tray to put the clean rocks on. Are they drying on the tray?"*

- Have all sizes, shapes, and colors of seashells in the water along with pebbles.

GO FISHING: Cut out colored acetate fish from old report covers. Slip a metal clip onto each fish. Make several fishing poles with magnets at the end of the strings. Float the fish and let children go fishing. You might set several pails next to the water for the children to put their fish in. After fishing, have the children return their fish to the lake so someone else can go fishing.

STIR UP THE WATER: Add 2 or 3 objects at a time that can be used to agitate the water. You could have: an egg beater, dull metal fork, and a whisk; egg beater and flour sifter; or several basters and plastic eye droppers.

Encourage The Children: *"Jerlean, you and Billy sure look like you're having fun mixing up the water.*

TWO TUBS IN ONE: Get two large rubber wash tubs. Put both of them in the water table. Set up a variety of activities:

- **Back and Forth:** Fill one tub with water and set the second tub right next to it. Put measuring cups, small pitchers, large sponges, or several basters in the water table. Trying not to spill any water into the big water table, transfer the water from one tub to the other. Can you move it back again?

- **Find, Catch, and Lift:** In one tub put lots of rocks, marbles, buttons, or other objects which are small and sink. Fill that tub about half full of water. Have children find objects, catch them with the tongs, lift them out of the water, and set them in the second tub.
  VARIATION: To make this activity a little more difficult add about an inch of sand to the first tub. To make it easier, add objects which float, such at ping pong balls.
  Encourage The Children: "Sarah, look at that marble you just put in the tub. What colors do you see?" "Cathy, you are really holding onto that rock. Good for you!"

- **Scrub and Rinse:** Have 5 or 6 large rocks and several fingernail or other small scrub brushes. Set them in the water table. Fill one tub with soap water and the second one with rinse water. Put a dish drainer next to the second tub. Have children scrub the rocks clean, rinse them off, and set them in the drainer to dry.
  Encourage The Children: "You are really cleaning that rock, Mary. I was watching you scrub that crack." "John, please help me change this rinse water. It seems to be getting too soapy. Thank you."

SINK THE SHIP: Cut styrofoam egg cartons into single and double cup pieces to make boats. Have several styrofoam meat trays. Put different size metal washers into a bowl.

Choose one of the 'boats' to float around your lake. Lay a washer on it. Is the boat still floating? Add another washer. Now what is the boat doing? Continue adding washers until you've sunk the ship.
Encourage The Children: "Sami, you're floating a big boat. Where are you going to put your first washer? Do you think your boat will sink? Try it, I'll watch."

BOAT FLOAT: Have a variety of objects available which children can use as boats, (sponges, jar lids, styrofoam trays, tree bark, paint stir sticks, tongue depressors, and large styrofoam packing molds).

- Float a large packing mold. Have miniature people and animals available.

- Have several jar lids in the water. Let children sail their boats by blowing them around the water.

- Add 'water lilies' to your lake. Using colored construction paper or shiny wrapping paper, cut out flowers using the pattern. Fold the four petals to the center. Put the square of paper in the water and let it float around. Soon you'll have colorful flowers floating in your lake. When the lilies absorb too much water and sink, take them out and float more.
  ~ thank you Kevin Carnes, Lakeshore Curriculum Materials

4"

4"

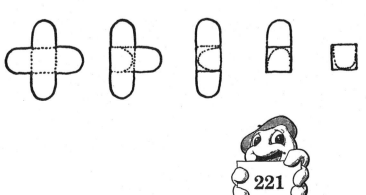

Outside

BATHING SUIT DAYS: Designate one day every couple of weeks as 'Bathing Suit Day'. Weather permitting fill several wading pools with water. Have the children wear their bathing suits and play in the water.

WASHING UP: Periodically have 'Wash-Up Days' at school. Have a large bucket of soapy water, sponges, and dry cloths. Bring out the objects which need washing such as chairs, dolls, cars, or riding toys. Wash the objects, rinse them off, dry them with the towels, and then let them dry further in the sun.

TRICKLING WATER: On warm days let the hose trickle a little water onto the play yard so that children can cool off and play in the water.

SNOW FUN: During the winter months play with snow both outside and inside. While outside enjoy building, molding, sculpting, and romping. When you come inside, bring some snow in with you and put it in the water table. Let the children wear mittens and play with it some more.

WE'RE FOREVER BLOWING BUBBLES: Create a variety of bubble blowing experiences for the children to do either inside or outside. Make **your** own bubble mixtures.

BUBBLE BREW I

You'll Need:
    Water
    Liquid Detergent

To Make: Pour the water into the container that you are going to use for blowing. Add a little liquid detergent. If you need more add it very gradually.

BUBBLE BREW II

You'll Need:
    1 Quart Water
    3/4 Cup Liquid Detergent
    (Joy or Dawn)
    1/4 Cup Corn Syrup

To Make: Let the children help you mix all of the ingredients together in a large bowl. Let it sit overnight. It will be ready to use the next day. Store any leftover bubble brew in a covered container in the refrigerator.

BUBBLE BREW III

You'll Need:
    2 Quarts Water
    1 Cup Liquid Detergent
    (Joy or Dawn)
    1 T Sugar
    2 T Glycerine

To Make: Let the children help you mix all of the ingredients in a large bowl. Cover it and let it stand for at least three hours. Store it in the refrigerator overnight.

INDIVIDUAL BUBBLE BLOWING: Give the children opportunities to blow bubbles with their own wands and blowers.

- Make an individual bubble blowing cup by inserting a wide plastic straw at an angle near the top of a styrofoam cup. Fill the cup about half full of water. Add a drop of liquid detergent and let the child blow. Refill as needed.

- Mix some bubble brew using recipe number 2 or 3. Pour it into small pitchers. Put the pitchers, 4 or 5 pie pans, and several types of bubble wands such as spoons or pancake turners with holes on the table or floor. When a child wants to make bubbles, he can pour some solution into a pie pan, choose a wand, and begin blowing.

GROUP BUBBLE BLOWING: Give the children opportunities to blow bubbles together.

- Get a huge container such as a wash tub. Fill it about half full of water. Add 3 or 4 squirts of liquid detergent. Give a wide mouth plastic straw to each child who would like to play. (Put his name on his straw or be sure to throw straws away after each use.)

  Children can stand around the tub and blow, blow, blow! Soon bubbles will appear and then rise up, up, up and maybe even spill over the top.

- Mix some bubble brew using recipe number 2 or 3. Pour it into a large, flat container such as a brownie pan. Have several types of wands available from which the children can choose, (single-sided cheese graters, clean fly swatters, colanders, funnels, apple slicers, berry baskets, 6 or 8 pack soda plastic).

  Lay the container of bubble solution in an open area and let the children dip their wands into the solution and then wave them up high. Where did the bubbles go? How big/small were they? What colors do you see? Can you catch any of the bubbles? Be gentle.

... notes for myself ~

ADDITIONAL RESOURCES

- **Creative Curriculum,** *Dodge.* Seven learning centers including sand.
- **Outside Play and Learning,** *Miller.* Variety of outdoor activities including sand and water, plus language, science, art, and more.
- **Sift and Shout,** *Granovetter/Jones.* Sand activities for a large tub, sand table, or outdoor sand box.
- **Waterworks,** *James/Granovetter.* Water activities for pitchers, tubs, buckets, and the water table.

Science

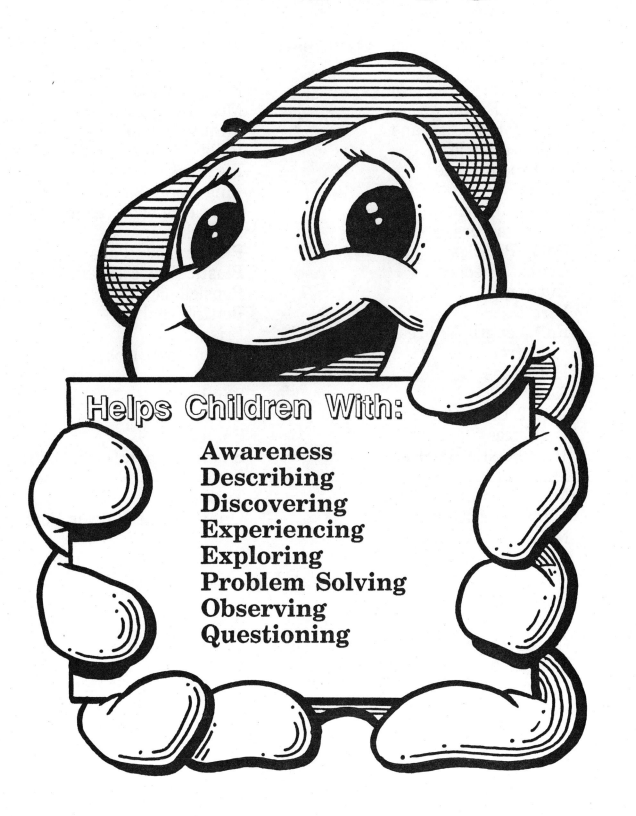

Helps Children With:

Awareness
Describing
Discovering
Experiencing
Exploring
Problem Solving
Observing
Questioning

Science

Supply List

Accessories

Aquarium
Artificial Flowers
Automobile Oil Pans
Balance Scale
Bathroom Scale
Bulbs
Clear Unbreakable
    Containers
Color Paddles
Cookie Sheets
Cuttings
Dirt
Full Length Unbreakable
    Mirror
Hourglass
Keys
1 or 2 Liter Plastic
    Bottles
16oz Plastic Bottles
Magnets
Magnet Wands
Magnifying Glass
Measuring Cups

Measuring Spoons
Measuring Pitchers
Minute Timer
Pails
Pie Pans
Ping Pong Balls
Plastic Spoons, Knives,
    Forks
Plastic Dish Tubs
Plastic Trays (Large)
Popsicle Sticks
Potting Soil
Prisms
Resonator Blocks
Rocks
Sand
Seeds
Shells
Small Garden Tools
Stool
Tweezers
Unbreakable Flower Pots

Clean-Up

Brooms
Cloths
Dustpans

Sponges
Waste Basket
Water

Dirt

DIRT MIX AND MATCH: Pour dirt into your sand/water table and give the children many opportunities to use it with and without accessories.

- Have the children sift dirt through their fingers, pile it up, build mountains, dig trenches, push it around, poke holes, and examine it. *Encourage The Children: Ask the children how the dirt feels, if they like building with it, what they are digging, and so on.*

- Put a spray bottle filled with a little water in the sand/water table. Let the children moisten the dirt and play. *Encourage The Children: "Mario, how does the wet dirt feel?" "Sabrina, is wet dirt easier to mold than dry dirt?"*

- Have tweezers, popsicle sticks, plastic knives, forks, and spoons, and several magnifying glasses in the dirt. Let the children examine the dirt carefully. They can put a little on a spoon to look at with a magnifying glass, carefully separate clumps and see if there are small twigs, stones, or other objects in the dirt, or put a small clump on the palm of their hand and very gently separate it with a fork.

- Have garden tools, flower pots, and small artificial flowers with the dirt.

DIRT SHAKE: Spoon 2 to 3 inches of dirt into a 2 liter plastic bottle and then fill it about 1/3 full with water. Have the children shake it up and watch it settle -- shake and watch -- shake and watch.

Once the children are familiar with how the dirt looks, add things from nature which are normally found in dirt, such as a leaf, a stone, a stick, grass, a nut, etc. Now have the children shake and watch the bottle. Can they find the objects you've added? Are they floating?
Encourage The Children: Have the children shake the bottle very slowly, rock it from side to side, swirl it, roll it, turn it upside down, and so on. Watch what happens to the dirt, to the water, and to the objects.

MAKE MUDPIES: Pour dirt into a plastic dish tub. Have a pitcher of water and a sturdy stick or spoon. Pour a little water into the dirt and mix it around. See if you can mold mudpies. Add more water if you need to. Set the 'mud' on a table. Put a cookie sheet next to it. Let the children make mudpies and set them on the cookie sheet. When they've finished, put the cookie sheet on the window ledge to bake. Watch the mudpies. What is happening to them? After awhile take the mudpies outside and crumble the dirt back up into the grass or garden.

Water

IN THE BOTTLE: Save 16oz, and 1 and 2 liter plastic bottles with their caps. Fill them with different liquids and objects for the children to shake, swirl, tilt, and watch.

- **Color Bottles:** Fill several 16oz bottles about 2/3 full with clear water. Slowly add a different food coloring to each bottle. Watch the coloring mix with the water. After a minute or so, cap the bottle and gently shake it until the food coloring has completely mixed with the water. Put the color bottles on a small table.
  Encourage The Children: Have the children shake the bottles. "Ali, look at the green water. What happened when you shook it? Shake it again. Look carefully and stop shaking as soon as you see the bubbles starting. Shake it really fast. Can you make lots of air bubbles?"

- **Oily Bottles:** Make color bottles as you did above. Add a little vegetable oil to each one.
  Encourage The Children: "Mo, can you shake the bottle really fast?" "Terrence, turn the bottle on its side and very gently rock it back and forth." "Junior, turn your yellow bottle upside down. How does the water look?"

- **Sponge Bottles:** Cut up different colored sponges into small pieces. Fill a 2 liter bottle about half full of water. Drop the sponges into the bottle. Watch them float and swim around.
  EXTENSION: Every night take the sponges out of the bottle to dry up. Let the children put them back in the next day. Watch the sponges as they expand.
  Encourage The Children: Ask children to find different colored sponges floating in the water. "Sharon, where's the pink sponge?" "Kevin, do you see the blue sponge? Where is it exactly? Shake up the bottle and let's see if the blue sponge swims to a different place. Did it?"

 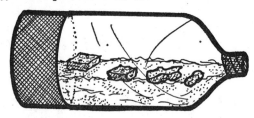

- **Sink and Float Bottles:** Fill a 2 liter bottle to the top with clear water. Place a glass eyedropper which has a rubber bulb into the bottle, bulb up. Tightly screw the cap on and then wrap masking tape around the cap for additional safety.
  The eyedropper should float at the top of the bottle. Squeeze the sides of the bottle and watch the dropper. Release the sides of the bottle. Watch the dropper.

- **Double Bottles:** Get two, 2 liter bottles and a one inch diameter piece of vinyl pipe. (plumbing supplies) Fill one bottle with clear or colored water. Drop a small object such as a die, coin, or toothpick into the water. Connect the two bottles together by screwing the tops into the ends of the vinyl pipe.

    Have a children turn the full bottle over, hold onto it, and watch the water flow into the empty bottle.
    EXTENSION: Have bottle races. Make several double bottles, each with the same amount of water but a different object. Say "1,2,3 turn your bottles over." The children turn their bottles over, hold onto them, and watch which one empties first.
    Encourage The Children: "Ashwini, what is happening to the water?" Tilt the bottle. "What is happening to the water now?" Watch the toothpick. "What is it doing? Does it flow into the empty bottle along with the water?" Swirl the bottle. "What is happening to the water this time?"

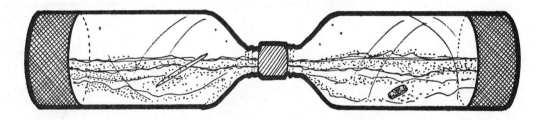

WAIT AND WATCH: Use water in different states to give the children opportunities to see it from liquid to solid.

- Put a pie pan on the table. Using a permanent marker, make a water line on the inside of the pan. Let a child pour water into the pan, right up to the line. Carefully carry it over to the window ledge and set it down. Check the water when you pass by the ledge.
    Encourage The Children: Talk about the amount of water in the pan. Someday it will be empty. Where do the children think the water might have gone?

- Just before it's going to rain, put a bucket or tub outside. After the rain is over, bring the bucket/tub inside. See how full it is.

- Put several trays of ice cubes into a brownie pan. Set the pan on a low table. Watch what happens to the cubes.

- Get several identical containers such as rubber dish tubs. Fill each with the same amount of snow. Bring them inside and place them in different areas of the room such as near a sunny window, on a table, and in the refrigerator. Keep your eye on them. What's happening?

- If it begins to hail, quickly put a container outside to catch some of the stones.

Magnets

MAGNET SURVEY: Hang a magnet over a table. Set two pans on the table for sorting - an aluminum cookie sheet for the non-magnetic objects and an automobile oil pan for the magnetic things. Have the children bring objects from around the room over to the table. Touch each object to the magnet. If it is attracted, put the object on the oil pan; if it is not, set it on the cookie sheet.

Encourage The Children: *"Blanca, you've got a wooden block. Do you think that it will stick to the magnet? I'll watch you try. No it didn't magnetize. Put it on the cookie sheet." "Michelle, you've brought three objects. Do you think any of them will be attracted? Which ones?"*

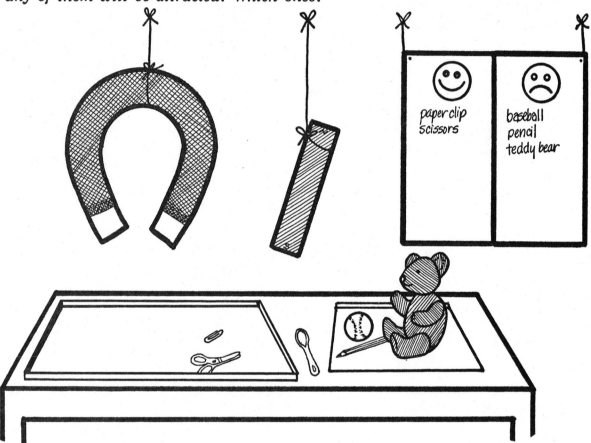

paper clip
scissors

baseball
pencil
teddy bear

CAPTURE THE CLIPS: Fill a tub about half full of sand. Mix in lots of metal paper clips. Have several magnetic wands near the tub. Let the children wave the wands across the sand and pick up paper clips. Take the captured clips off the wand and put them in a small container. Mix up the sand a little and wave the wand across the top again to capture more clips. Continue until all of the clips have been captured.

EXTENSION: Other times you set up this activity mix different objects with the sand such as metal washers, nails, screws, keys, ball bearings, and magnetic bingo chips.

Five Senses

SEEING: Set up a variety of activities to encourage the children to use their eyes.

- **Sight Tray:** Get a large tray. Put a variety of things on the tray which people use to help protect their eyes or to see better. For example you could have safety goggles, a telescope, a pair of glasses, a magnifying glass, a pair of binoculars, and a swimming mask. You could also have a picture of a guide dog.

- **Sight Tray II:** Put 7-8 objects (pencil, flower, small piece of carpeting, a rock, a leaf, a colorful picture, a catalogue) on a tray plus several magnifying glasses. Have the children use the magnifying glasses to look at each of the objects more closely.
  Encourage The Children: "Jamaal, what colors do you see when you look carefully at the leaf? Oh, you see red, black, and brown. Look again and see if there are any other colors. You also see yellow." "Betty, do the letters in the catalogue get bigger and smaller as you move the magnifying glass closer and further away from the page?"

- **Observation Tower:** Put a stool by a window so that children can easily watch what is going on outside. Add binoculars from time to time.

- **Make A Mobile:** Gather lots of different cardboard tubes from wrapping paper, paper towels, and toilet tissue. Have the children paint them with either one color such as white or different colors. After the tubes have dried, assemble them into a giant mobile for the classroom.

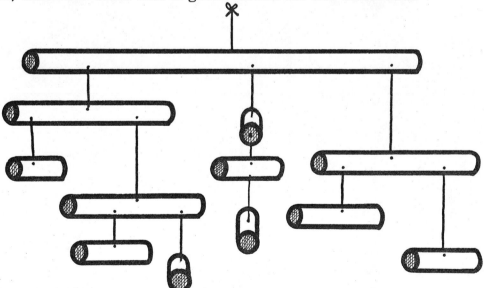

- **Watch Carefully:** Set several different hour glass timers on the table. Turn them over and watch the sand drain to the other side. Do it again.

TOUCHING: Set up a variety of activities to encourage the children to use their sense of touch.

- **Touching Tray:** Put 7-8 objects which have different textures on a tray. (brick, sponge ball, bark, corrugated cardboard, velvet, piece of pegboard, giant screw, beaded mat, piece of artificial turf)
  Encourage The Children: "Sherita, did you touch the bark on both sides? Did they feel the same?" "Greg, you're pressing your fingers into the holes on the pegboard. Having fun? Good!"

- **Prickly-Tickly:** Have a big basket with two types of objects in it, one that's rough or prickly (sandpaper, toothpick, nail, emery board, pencil, buckle, screw, piece of a door mat) and the other that's soft and tickly (fur, cotton, teddy bear, pom-pom, yarn, rabbit's foot, velvet). Duplicate the teddy bear and cactus and make a simple sorting board like the one illustrated. Let children feel each object and decide if it is prickly or tickly and then set it on the board.

- **Cornstarch Touch:** Pour a cup of cornstarch into a large flat pan with shallow sides. Have a cup of water in a pitcher. Let a child pour a little water into the pan. (It is a fairly dry mixture.) Using their fingers let the children gently push the water and cornstarch together. Add a little more water as needed.

HEARING: Set up a variety of activities to encourage the children to use their ears.

- **Hearing Tray:** Put 7-8 objects which make a sound and are common to the children's environment on a tray, (alarm clock, egg timer, clicker, telephone, bell, horn, buzzer, radio, tape recorder, record player). Let the children explore.
  Encourage The Children: *"Sam, what kind of sound does your telephone make at home when it rings?" "Rich, do you have a radio at your home? What do you like to listen to?"*

- **Listen Carefully:** Put a set of containers on the table, such as different size pans or metal buckets. Have a rubber, metal, plastic, and wooden spoon. Tap the containers with each of the spoons. Listen carefully. Do you hear different sounds?
  Encourage The Children: *Tell a child to cover his eyes. You pick up a spoon and gently tap several containers while the child listens. Ask him if he knows which type of spoon you're tapping with.*

- **Play Music:** Set out musical instruments which are different than your regular classroom instruments but which are easy to play, such as a washboard, xylophone, or guitar (one type at a time). Let the children experiment with the different sounds each one can make.
  EXTENSION: Make different instruments which the children can use to further explore different sounds. For example, get 5-6 different size pieces of wood and lay them on a thick towel. Have a large wooden spoon. Play the blocks. Get a metal loaf pan and brownie pan. Stretch 4-5 rubber bands around each one. Pluck those bands. Get a set of resonator blocks and a mallet. Set two or three blocks out and let the children experiment.

- **Where's The Timer:** Have a minute timer which makes a loud buzz. Turn it to go off in five or six minutes. Without anyone seeing you, hide it someplace in the room. When it goes off, have everyone listen and figure out where it is. Check out the places that the children suggest until you've found it.

- **Freeze and Listen:** Periodically during your free choice time call out, "Freeze (pause) and listen." The children should stop what they are doing and listen for sounds around them. Let them name sounds they hear and then go back to their play.

TASTING: Set up a variety of activities to encourage the children to use their sense of taste.

- **Tasting Tray:** For several weeks offer the children different samples of foods to taste. For example cut up several types of bread such as sweet bread, sour dough, and bagels. Put the pieces in muffin cups and let the children taste the different breads. Talk about how the breads taste. On other days cut up fruits, vegetables, and cheeses. Try different crackers. It is fun to taste the differences between salted and unsalted foods such as butter, pretzels, crackers, peanuts, cottage cheese, and so on. Try sweetened and non-sweetened foods such as a variety of plain and frosted cereals.

- **Make Butter:** Get a small carton of whipping cream and several small plastic jars with lids, such as the ones from peanut butter or mayonnaise. Pour several teaspoons of cream into each of the jars. Have children sit in pairs across from each other and roll the jars back and forth over the floor. After 15-20 minutes the cream will begin to harden and form a solid. Pour off the excess liquid. Add a little salt if you'd like. Enjoy tasting your butter on pieces of rye bread.

- **Growing Sprouts:** Get some alfalfa or radish seeds, a wide mouth jar, a piece of cheesecloth, and a rubber band. Measure 1T of seeds and put them in the jar. Fill the jar about half full of warm water. Cover the jar with the cloth and secure it with the rubber band. Soak overnight.

  The next day, leave the cheesecloth on the jar and drain the water out. Fill the jar with more lukewarm water, swirl it around to rinse the seeds and drain again. Let the jar rest upside down in a dish drainer. Rinse again during the day and then let it drain upside down overnight. Repeat the rinsing process twice a day until the seeds sprout.

  When the sprouts are ready, make 'sprout roll-ups' by putting small bunches of sprouts in the middle of lettuce leaves and rolling them up. Enjoy the taste.

SMELLING: Set up a variety of activities to encourage the children to use their nose.

- **Smelling Tray:** Get 6 to 8 film canisters. Poke a wad of cotton into each one. Pour a drop or two of a different extract onto each piece of cotton. (lemon, vanilla, spearmint, peppermint, almond, cinnamon, etc.) Poke several small holes in each cap and cover the canisters. Put them on a tray. Set the tray on a table so that the children can easily smell each of canisters.
  VARIATION: Instead of using extracts, use spices (pepper, bay leaves, mustard, etc.). Another time use different flavors of gelatin.
  EXTENSION: After the children are familiar with the different scents, make a duplicate set of 'smelling jars' and put them on the tray. Let the children pair the matching jars.

- **Smell It:** Duplicate the clown face as many times as you'd like. Cut them out and tape them to different things in your classroom. (blocks, chair, vase, blackboard, door, table, etc.) As the children are playing in the room, have them also look for clown faces. When someone finds a face, he can smell the object.

- **Hide A Smell:** Purposefully prepare snacks which have a familiar smell. (peanut butter/crackers, orange wedges, bowl of popcorn) While the children are out of the room, cover the snack and hide it. When they return, talk about what the children think the familiar smell is, and then search for the snack. Enjoy eating.

Shadows

SHADOW, SHADOW EVERYWHERE: On sunny days take every opportunity to find and talk about shadows.

- On neighborhood walks search the sidewalk for shadows of trees, fire hydrants, and so on.

- In the classroom see if there are any shadows flashing on your walls or floors.

- On the playground encourage the children to find their own shadows and those of playground equipment.

ME AND MY SHADOW: Duplicate the 'shadow cards' and mount them on a piece of colored construction paper. Hang the shadow poster next to your full length mirror. Let the children look at the shadows on the cards and copy them.

Encourage The Children: "Erika, which shadow are you pretending to be? Oh, you're making up your own shadows. Right now you look like a jumping shadow." "Jon, you've been over here a long time. Are you pretending to be every shadow on the chart?"

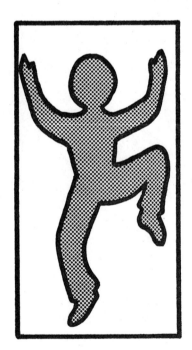
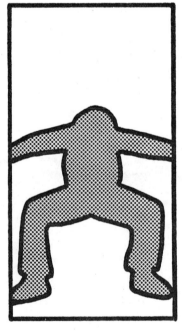

238

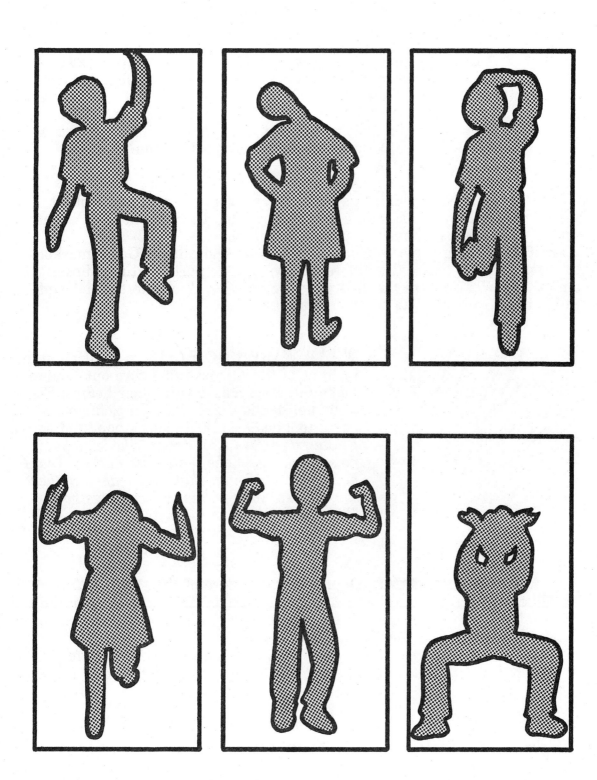

Know Your Body

NAME MY PARTS: Duplicate the picture of the children on page 241 and glue it to construction paper. Hang the poster near your full length mirror. Have a child look at the poster and point to a body part on the picture and then point to his own body. If two or more children are playing, let one child point to a body part on the picture and everyone point to the part on his own body. As children are pointing to their body parts, name them.

WHAT MOVES: Have children stand in front of the mirror and look at themselves. As they are standing there, encourage them to move different parts of their bodies. Name the parts that move.
EXTENSION: Hang a piece of posterboard near the mirror. Get a marker. Make an on-going list of the different moving body parts as the children name them. When you're finished with the activity, duplicate the list and send it home in your next parent newsletter.

WHAT MAKES NOISE: Have children stand in front of the mirror and figure out how to make different noises with their bodies. For example, hands - clap, feet - tap, fingers - snap, tongues - cluck, cheeks - pop, and so on.
Encourage The Children: "Sheila, what noises can you make with your hands? Yes, I hear them clapping. Can they make another sound? Yes, your palms can rub together." "Liz, you're clucking with your _____. Tell me what you are using to make that noise."

HOW ARE WE THE SAME: Duplicate the picture of the giraffe on page 242. Glue it to a piece of colored construction paper and hang it near the full length mirror. Have the children find one of the giraffe's body parts, such as his nose, and then find theirs. Find another one and so on.
Encourage The Children: "Jo, does the giraffe have a nose? Point to it. Do you have a nose? Do you think the noses look alike? How? Different? How?"

HOW TALL ARE YOU: Construct a four or five foot giraffe for your wall. Have the children stand next to it. Mark off on the giraffe how tall each child is.
EXTENSION: Have a bathroom scale near the giraffe. Weigh each child after measuring his height.
Encourage The Children: "Jack, look. You come up to the middle of the giraffe's neck!" "Sally, your hair touches the big brown spot on the giraffe."

Foods

TO EAT OR NOT TO EAT: Make food and non-food cards. To make the cards cut out magazine and catalogue pictures of food and non-food items. Glue each picture to an index card. Laminate or cover them with clear adhesive. Make a simple sorting board like the one illustrated.

Set the board and cards on a table. If the card is a picture of a food, put it on the smiley side; if not, put it on the frowning side.

YUM-YUM: Get models or pictures of food representing the main food groups. Put them in a large basket. Have a bread pan, salad bowl, roasting pan, and milk carton. Have a child pick up one of the foods and decide which container it should go into. Put it there. Continue naming and sorting the other foods.
Encourage The Children: "Jackson, you're holding a piece of bread. Do you think that it should go into the bread pan, salad bowl, roasting pan, or milk carton? Why?"

EXPLORE A FOOD: Put several apples on a tray. Let the children look at, feel, and smell them. Talk with the children as they examine the apples. After several days, bring a knife to the table and carefully cut one or two apples in half. (Remember safety.) What do the children see? Let the children examine the apple halves. You might even add a magnifying glass to the tray so that the children can look more closely at the stems, seeds, cores, etc.
EXTENSION: On each of the days that the children are examining the apple, have different apple snacks, such as fresh wedges, apple cider, applesauce, apple pie, apple coffee cake, etc.

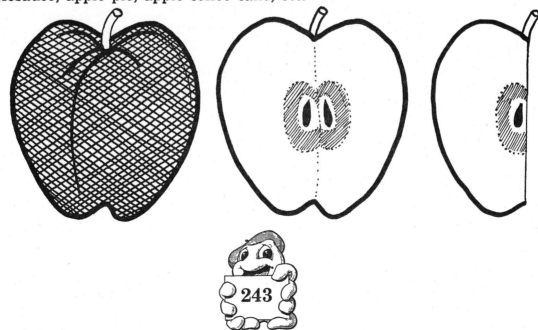

Colors

COLOR PADDLES: Get a set of plastic color paddles or cut sheets of different colored acetate from report covers. Set the colors in a sunny window. Have the children hold them up and look at the colors. Combine different colors. What new colors can the children discover?

COLOR BOTTLES: Make eight or more 16oz bottles of colored water. Put out one color for the children to look at. The next day add a second color, and so on until the entire set is out for the children to examine.
Encourage The Children: "Samantha, look at the green bottle. Now hold it up to the light and look at it again. Does the color look the same?"

BAG OF COLOR: Make this colorful mixture and let your children squish and squash it around.

<u>You'll Need:</u>
1/3 Cup Sugar
1 Cup Cornstarch
4 Cups Cold Water
Food Coloring
1 Resealable Plastic Bag

<u>To Make:</u> Pour the first 3 ingredients into a pan. Stirring constantly, heat them until the mixture thickens. Cool.
Divide the mixture into 3 separate bowls. Add one color of food coloring to each container and mix. Spoon the colors into one plastic bag. Seal it and tape it closed for additional security.
from Mudpies to Magnets by Williams, Rockwell, and Sherwood

COLORED CUBES: Add food coloring to water to make colored ice cubes. Put them in a large clear container and watch them melt.
EXTENSION: Another time that you do this activity, make different colored ice cubes:

PURPLE = Red + Little Blue   GREEN = Yellow + Little Blue
ORANGE = Yellow + Little Red   BLACK = All 3 colors

PRISM WATCH: Put several prisms on a ledge near a sunny window. Let the children flash rainbows on the walls and ceiling.

Rocks and Shells

BALANCING ACT: Set the balance scale on a table along with a container of different size rocks and another container with different shells. Have the children mix and match the rocks and shells trying to balance the two sides.

SORT THE ROCKS: Have two or three pieces of heavy, colored yarn and a container of different rocks or shells. Tie each piece of yarn together to form two or three circles. Have a child look at all of the rocks/shells and figure out how he wants to sort them (by color, size, texture, points, curves, etc.). Look at each rock/shell and decide which yarn circle it should go into. Look at the next rock/shell and decide. Let him continue until he has sorted all of the rocks/shells.
Encourage The Children: As children are sorting talk with them about why they are putting a certain rock/shell with a group.

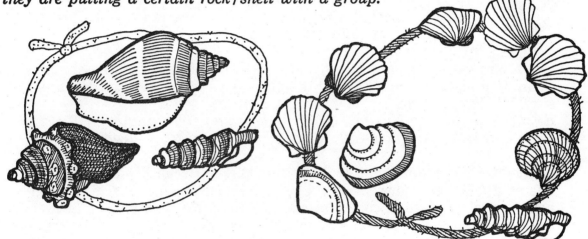

LOOK CAREFULLY: Display 7-8 rocks or shells on a clear non-breakable tray along with several magnifying glasses. Have the children use their senses as they examine each rock/shell.
EXTENSION: Put a bowl of water on the tray. Let the children examine the rocks/shells when they are wet. Any similarities? Differences?
Encourage The Children: "Jeff, which rocks feel bumpy to you? Did you look at them with the magnifying glass? Did you see the little holes?"

Planting

CLASSROOM GARDENS: Give the children ongoing experiences with growing grasses, vegetables, flowers, and plants.

- In the Fall plant flower bulbs near your school. Watch for them to grow in the Spring.

- Let the children start flowers from seeds. Give the children small cups. Let them spoon some dirt into their cups and then sprinkle a few seeds on top. Gently poke the seeds under the dirt. Let each child water his own seeds. Put the cups on a tray and set them in a sunny window. Turn them every day or so and keep them moist.

  Watch. Soon they will begin to sprout. When they seem sturdy and the weather is appropriate, plant your flower seedlings outside.

- Get a large shallow pan. Fill it about half full of dirt. Let the children sprinkle grass seed on it. Spray it lightly with water. Place it in the sunlight. Keep it moist.

  Encourage The Children: *"Samuel, where do you think we will see grass come up first?" "Asi, how tall do you think our grass will grow?"*

- Gather several plants that grow from cuttings. Break a piece from each one at a joint. Get several clear plastic bags or cups. Put a moistened paper towel or piece of cotton in each bag/cup. Put one cutting between the towel/cotton and the side of each the container. Set the cuttings on a tray. Put them in a warm place out of direct sunlight. Watch what happens to your cuttings. When the roots have formed, plant the new plants in flower pots. Keep them in the sun and water regularly.

Outside

WHILE OUTSIDE: While the children are outside, take advantage of the natural surroundings.

- Talk about the weather and the clothes that the children are wearing to protect themselves. You might even discuss sun protection with lotions and other items.

- Notice worms, ants, and other crawling creatures on walkways, driveways, buildings, etc. A good time to do this is when the children arrive, since the natural environment has not been disturbed by activity. Take magnifying glasses out with you so that the children can look at the crawling wildlife even more closely,

- Take lots of walks around the neighborhood. Watch the trees, flowers, and animals. Remember to look up. Keep track of the sky around you too. *Encourage The Children: Have the children listen for sounds. Do they hear waves, wind, leaves, chirping birds, or a breaking branch? Look at a nearby flag. Is it moving? How much? Why?*

- Make a special 'Collection Bag.' Take it with you when you are going to collect a certain object -- shells, feathers, rocks, leaves, sticks, nuts, seeds, and so on. Display the collection on a large tray when you return. Have a magnifying glass near the tray for even closer examination.

SKY VIEW: Using yarn and paper towel rolls let the children make telescopes. On a nice day, take the scopes with you outside. Let the children lie down on the ground and look at the sky through their telescopes. *Encourage The Children: "Chenault, what do you see through your telescope?" "Hallie, can you see that bird flying overhead?" "Let's all look at the clouds. Are they moving? What do they look like to you?"*

NATURE WEAVING: Using two tree branches or dowel rods and heavy string make a simple loom. Collect pussy willows, corn stalks, weeds, long sticks with leaves, etc. Starting at the bottom, weave the nature through the strings. Continue weaving until the hanging is full. Hang it in a prominent place for everyone to see.

OUR TREE: Pick a tree which is very close to school and easily accessible. Once every week or two, visit the tree and carefully look at it. Start near the bottom. Look at the roots if they are showing through the soil. Note the bark. How does it feel? Keep looking up the trunk of the tree. See what is happening to the branches. What is at the very top of your tree?

Now look more closely. Are any animals making homes in your tree? Look for holes, webs, and nests. Use a magnifying glass to examine the bark. Anything crawling around?

As time goes on note how your tree changes. What about the leaves? Bark? Animal homes? Creatures?

... *notes for myself* ~

ADDITIONAL RESOURCES

- **Bubbles, Rainbows, and Worms,** *Brown.* Beginning science activities.
- **Hug A Tree,** *Williams/Rockwell/Sherwood.* Outdoor science activities.
- **Instant Curriculum,** *Shiller/Rossano.* 9 curriculum areas, including science.
- **More Mudpies To Magnets,** *Williams/Rockwell/Sherwood.* Activities for the five senses, colors, water, dirt, health, and more.
- **Mudpies To Magnets,** *Williams/Rockwell/Sherwood.* Activities for How Things Work, Earth, Weather, Plants, and more.
- **Our World,** *Bittinger.* Activities to help children care for the land, air, and water around them.

BUILDING BLOCKS Library

The Circle Time Series

by Liz and Dick Wilmes. Hundreds of activities for large and small groups of children. Each book is filled with Language and Active games, Fingerplays, Songs, Stories, Snacks, and more. A great resource for every library shelf.

Circle Time Book
Captures the spirit of 39 holidays and seasons.
ISBN 0-943452-00-7   **$ 12.95**

Everyday Circle Times
Over 900 ideas. Choose from 48 topics divided into 7 sections: self-concept, basic concepts, animals, foods, science, occupations, and recreation.
ISBN 0-943452-01-5   **$16.95**

More Everyday Circle Times
Divided into the same 7 sections as EVERYDAY. Features new topics such as Birds and Pizza, plus all new ideas for some popular topics contained in EVERYDAY.
ISBN 0-943452-14-7   **$16.95**

Yearful of Circle Times
52 different topics to use weekly, by seasons, or mixed throughout the year. New Friends, Signs of Fall, Snowfolk Fun, and much more.
ISBN 0-943452-10-4   **$16.95**

Paint Without Brushes

by Liz and Dick Wilmes. Use common materials which you already have. Discover the painting possibilities in your classroom! PAINT WITHOUT BRUSHES gives your children open-ended art activities to explore paint in lots of creative ways. A valuable art resource. One you'll want to use daily.
ISBN 0-943452-15-5   **$12.95**

Easel Art

by Liz & Dick Wilmes. Let the children use easels, walls, outside fences, clip boards, and more as they enjoy the variety of art activities filling the pages of EASEL ART. A great book to expand young children's art experiences.
ISBN 0-943452-25-2   **$ 12.95**

Everyday Bulletin Boards

by Wilmes and Moehling. Features borders, murals, backgrounds, and other open-ended art to display on your bulletin boards. Plus board ideas with patterns, which teachers can make and use to enhance their curriculum.
ISBN 0-943452-09-0   **$ 12.95**

Exploring Art

by Liz and Dick Wilmes. EXPLORING ART is divided by months. Over 250 art ideas for paint, chalk, doughs, scissors, and more. Easy to set-up in your classroom.
ISBN 0-943452-05-8   **$19.95**

Magnet Board Fun

by Liz and Dick Wilmes. Every classroom has a magnet board, every home a refrigerator. MAGNET BOARD FUN is crammed full of games, songs, and stories for your home and classroom. Hundreds of patterns to reproduce, color, and use immediately.
ISBN 0-943452-28-7 **$16.95**

Parachute Play

by Liz and Dick Wilmes. A year 'round approach to one of the most versatile pieces of large muscle equipment. Starting with basic techniques, PARACHUTE PLAY provides over 100 activities to use with your parachute.
ISBN 0-943452-03-1 **$ 9.95**

Activities Unlimited

by Adler, Caton, and Cleveland. Hundreds of innovative activities to help your children develop fine and gross motor skills, increase their language, become self-reliant, and play cooperatively. Whether you're a beginning teacher or a veteran, this book will quickly become one of your favorites.
ISBN 0-943452-17-1 **$16.95**

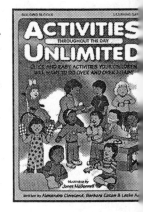

Felt Board Fingerplays

by Liz and Dick Wilmes. Over fifty popular fingerplays, each with full-size patterns. All accompanied by games and activities. Divided by seasons, this book is a quick reference for a year full of fingerplay fun.
ISBN 0-943452-26-0 **$16.95**

Felt Board Fun

by Liz and Dick Wilmes. Make your felt board come alive. Discover how versatile it is as the children become involved with a wide range of activities. This unique book has over 150 ideas with accompanying patterns.
ISBN 0-943452-02-3 **$16.95**

Table & Floor Games

by Liz and Dick Wilmes. 32 easy-to-make, fun-to-play table/floor games with accompanying patterns ready to trace or photocopy. Teach beginning concepts such as matching, counting, colors, alphabet, sorting and so on.
ISBN 0-943452-16-3 **$19.95**

Learning Centers

by Liz and Dick Wilmes. Hundreds of open-ended activities to quickly involve and excite your children. You'll use it every time you plan and whenever you need a quick, additional activity. A must for every teacher's bookshelf.
ISBN 0-943452-13-9 **$19.95**

Play With Big Boxes

by Liz and Dick Wilmes. Children love big boxes. Turn them into boats, telephone booths, tents, and other play areas. Bring them to art and let children collage, build, and paint them. Use them in learning centers for games, play stages, quiet spaces, puzzles, and more, more, more.
ISBN 0-943452-23-6 **$ 12.95**

Play With Small Boxes

by Liz and Dick Wilmes. Small boxes are free, fun, and provide unlimited possibilities. Use them for telephones, skates, scoops, pails, beds, buggies, and more. So many easy activities, you'll want to use small boxes every day.
ISBN 0-943452-24-4 **$ 12.95**

2's Experience Series

by Liz and Dick Wilmes. An exciting series developed especially for toddlers and twos!

's Experience - Art
Scribble, Paint, Smear, Mix, Tear, Mold, Taste, and more. Over 150 activities, plus lots of recipes and hints.
ISBN 0-943452-21-X **$16.95**

's Experience - Dramatic Play
Dress up and pretend! Hundreds of imaginary characters... fire-fighters, campers, bus drivers, and more.
ISBN 0-943452-20-1 **$12.95**

's Experience - Felt Board Fun
Make your felt board come alive. Enjoy stories, activities, and rhymes developed just for very young children. Hundreds of extra large patterns feature teddy bears, birthdays, farm animals, and much, much more.
ISBN 0-943452-19-8 **$14.95**

2's Experience - Fingerplays
A wonderful collection of easy fingerplays with accompanying games and large FINGERPLAY CARDS.
ISBN 0-943452-18-X **$12.95**

2's Experience - Sensory Play
Hundreds of playful, multi-sensory activities to encourage children to look, listen, taste, touch, and smell.
ISBN 0-943452-22-8 **$14.95**

TODDLERS & TWO'S

BUILDING BLOCKS Subscription	**$20.00**
2's EXPERIENCE Series	
2'S EXPERIENCE - ART	16.95
2'S EXPERIENCE - DRAMATIC PLAY	12.95
2'S EXPERIENCE - FELTBOARD FUN	14.95
2'S EXPERIENCE - FINGERPLAYS	12.95
2'S EXPERIENCE - SENSORY PLAY	14.95
CIRCLE TIME Series	
CIRCLE TIME BOOK	12.95
EVERYDAY CIRCLE TIMES	16.95
MORE EVERYDAY CIRCLE TIMES	16.95
YEARFUL OF CIRCLE TIMES	16.95
ART	
EASEL ART	12.95
EVERYDAY BULLETIN BOARDS	12.95
EXPLORING ART	19.95
PAINT WITHOUT BRUSHES	12.95
LEARNING GAMES & ACTIVITIES	
ACTIVITIES UNLIMITED	16.95
FELT BOARD FINGERPLAYS	16.95
FELT BOARD FUN	16.95
LEARNING CENTERS	19.95
MAGNET BOARD FUN	16.95
PARACHUTE PLAY	9.95
PLAY WITH BIG BOXES	12.95
PLAY WITH SMALL BOXES	12.95
TABLE & FLOOR GAMES	19.95

Prices subject to change without notice.

All books available from full-service book stores, educational stores, and school supply catalogs.